I am writing this letter to extend my support and endorsement to Stracey Grenville for her book "The Mind Matters".
I can confidently say that this book will be a success based on its content.

Dr. Wedlan Sealey, Apostle SOHP Kingdom Ministries

I am delighted to endorse Stracey Grenville book "The Mind Matters" After reading the manuscript, I am fully convinced that this book will be an asset to anyone who may choose to read it.

Leon Bogle Senior Pastor of "I am Blessed Ministries"

THE MIND
MATTERS

STRACEY GRENVILLE

WESTBOW
PRESS®
A DIVISION OF THOMAS NELSON
& ZONDERVAN

Copyright © 2022 Stracey Grenville.

All rights reserved. No part of this book may be used or reproduced by any means, graphic, electronic, or mechanical, including photocopying, recording, taping or by any information storage retrieval system without the written permission of the author except in the case of brief quotations embodied in critical articles and reviews.

This book is a work of non-fiction. Unless otherwise noted, the author and the publisher make no explicit guarantees as to the accuracy of the information contained in this book and in some cases, names of people and places have been altered to protect their privacy.

WestBow Press books may be ordered through booksellers or by contacting:

WestBow Press
A Division of Thomas Nelson & Zondervan
1663 Liberty Drive
Bloomington, IN 47403
www.westbowpress.com
844-714-3454

Because of the dynamic nature of the Internet, any web addresses or links contained in this book may have changed since publication and may no longer be valid. The views expressed in this work are solely those of the author and do not necessarily reflect the views of the publisher, and the publisher hereby disclaims any responsibility for them.

Any people depicted in stock imagery provided by Getty Images are models, and such images are being used for illustrative purposes only. Certain stock imagery © Getty Images.

Scripture taken from the King James Version of the Bible.

ISBN: 978-1-6642-5939-3 (sc)
ISBN: 978-1-6642-5937-9 (hc)
ISBN: 978-1-6642-5938-6 (e)

Library of Congress Control Number: 2022903884

Print information available on the last page.

WestBow Press rev. date: 03/15/2022

DEDICATION

This book is dedicated to my children, Kencey and Kasey and also my siblings who played a significant role in the completion of this book. None of this was possible without your love, support and encouragement. Thank you, my family.

Dr. Wedlan Sealey, apostle of SOPH Kingdom Ministries and Leon Bogle, senior pastor of I Am Blessed Ministries

ACKNOWLEDGEMENT

I give God the glory for the many people he has sent to help me along the way. This includes Pastor Leon Bogle, Dr. Wedlan Sealey, Dr. Virgina Sealey, Pastor Clavis Duke, Pastor Ann Duke, Pastor Jumu Grant and Pastor Ingrid Belle.

Measureless credit is extended to my friends, Joy, Symone, Colette, Veronica, Weslyn, Audrey and the Women of "I Am Blessed Ministries" and all of the many other people who would have encouraged me during this journey. These individuals are too numerous to mention, and I am forever grateful.

CONTENTS

Acknowledgement vii

Introduction xi

Chapter 1　The Power of the Mind 1

Chapter 2　Sound Knowledge Is Power 15

Chapter 3　The Biggest Threat to My Prosperity Could Be Me 28

Chapter 4　Bringing the Mind into Maturity. 37

Chapter 5　The Battle for the Soul 44

Chapter 6　The Toxic Mindset 63

Chapter 7　The Cultured Mindset 72

Chapter 8　The Fears of Confrontation 79

Chapter 9　The Mind of Christ toward You 90

INTRODUCTION

This book was written with you in mind; it is relevant and ideal for this time. Chaos, drama, challenges, and confusion are going on in the world, yet you still have to dream big, fulfill your purpose, and set goals and focus on reaching them to be successful. In all of this, what matters the most is your mindset—you can become either a victim or a victor. You can either lose hope or find hope *The Mind Matters* will help you to understand that a successful and prosperous life depends on how well you manage your mind. The manifestation of your outer life is a reflection of your inner life.

The *soul*, a term that is use interchangeably with the mind, is made up of the mind, will, and emotion. Our choices, decision-making, preferences, and the way we think and feel are seated in our souls. Bad choices can ruin our lives—politicians' bad decisions can throw a country into chaos; our own decisions can lock or unlock our purposes. In addition, the way we think will either progress or regress us, and our feelings toward a situation or circumstance will determine our responses, whether positive or negative. That is why the mind matters, and we need to be mindful of that because it determines whether we rise up or fall down.

The Mind Matters will help you to become aware of your mind's positive capability, as well as the damage it can cause if not managed properly. This book also will expose you to the nourishment and training you need to sustain vitality and productivity of the mind.

The mind really matters because it manages everything about us. We must be aware of the opposition and pitfalls that seek to detour us from managing our minds and prevent us from reaching our fullest potential.

Your mind is trainable; it is like a muscle. When you give it the right nourishment, and you train it for optimism, confidence, integrity, and empowerment, it will develop and become what it was trained to be

Psalm 139:14 tells us, "I will praise thee; for I am fearfully and wonderfully made: marvellous are thy works; and that my soul knoweth right well." Positive thoughts, optimistic feelings, and energy require the endorsement of your soul. When your soul is convinced, it validates your self-worth and, in doing so, chooses optimism over pessimism.

The way in which you value yourself will be determined by your mindset. When your mind has been convinced of who you are and what your capabilities are, no external voice can convince you otherwise. That is why the mind matters, and your participation and involvement gives it the opportunity to take you to the pinnacle of success.

CHAPTER 1

THE POWER OF THE MIND

The mind is a powerful tool because it can either keep you in bondage or liberate you. It has the power to reduce you to a state of distress or elevate you to the height of pleasure, allowing you to capitalize on its advantages.

The mind is a powerful tool and a gift from the Creator that human beings possess. It can be used to help you attain success, or it can take you to the depths of failure.

Every day when we wake up, we are faced with the responsibility of managing the day before us. The success of our days will determine how well we plan for them. We have to think, make decisions, and come up with suggestions and ideas so that every minute of the day will be accounted for. We plan ahead and then execute the plan afterward. It means our minds are like Energizer batteries—they keep going and going with little a chance to pause and no sleep because everything we do requires the application of our minds.

Consider Proverbs 13:4: "The soul of the sluggard desireth, and hath nothing but the soul of the diligent shall be made fat." I love this verse because it gives a clue to a successful life. What does this scripture say about our minds? How applicable is this scripture to a successful life? Remember, the soul is use interchangeably with *the mind*. Therefore, the scripture is saying that a lazy mind will bring poverty to our lives, and a diligent or hardworking mind will bring success to our lives. Poverty begins with a mindset, just as prosperity begins with a mindset. That is why 3 John 1:2 says, "Beloved I wish above all things that thou mayest prosper and be in good health as thy soul prospereth." The word *prosper* means to excel, succeed, and do well in every aspect of our lives. Here, we see that the prosperity of our lives is dependent on the prosperity of our minds, or our prosperous mindsets. Looking at the two scriptures, we see that to have a prosperous mindset, we must be diligent persons. The word *diligent* means hardworking, industrious, assiduous, persistent, and so forth. From these qualities comes the word *production*. That is why the scripture says the soul of the diligent shall be made fat. That is, if we use our mind effectively and efficiently, our lives will flourish; it will be fertile and it will be productive. We will be an asset that is having more than enough good things to impart and to share (become fat).

We can recognize that the scripture shows the correlation between abundance and a hardworking mind. Our minds are the key to our success; the mind is the unseen that produces the seen. In other words, our thinking could become something positive if we program our mind for success and allow it to manifest. Our achievements and accomplishments do not just happen; they begin with a thought that eventually becomes a reality. It is necessary to remind us, that the mind is the birthplace of our thought and so it means every good and bad things are birthed out of a thought. This means our thought can either work for us or work against us. This brings me to the point that our minds can react in either a positive or a negative way, taking us to the pinnacle of success or to the depths of regret. Our minds are very powerful and vital, and they serve as bridges to our destinies.

> **THE MIND IS THE UNSEEN THAT PRODUCES THE SEEN.**

Have you ever thought how important a bridge is when you want to go to the other side? The bridge is one of the means of taking you to your destination; similarly, so is the mind. Life is a journey; it is about movement. We are all going somewhere, but where we end up during and after our journey here on earth will be determined by the choices and the decisions we make during this time. It is for these reasons, we clearly see that the mind really matters.

THE MIND: A DECISION MAKER

We must reason or talk over some things before we make a final decision. Some decisions require consideration, deliberation, and scrutiny before we reach an answer. In a court of law, there is a moment of deliberation on the facts or arguments before reaching a final decision—the verdict. In these instances, the members of the jury would want to make the right decision, so they would discuss or have a conversation about the arguments put forward by both parties and ponder on it before coming up with a decision. This is meticulously done because someone's life may be on the line, and the court must uphold its integrity in keeping with the law of the land.

On the other hand, other decisions require not deliberation but instant obedience. For example, there are instances when God speaks to us through his words, people, dreams, and so on, giving us instructions to carry out a particular task. Instead of obeying the voice immediately, we might reason with our five senses, which allows us to see things from our own perspectives. Many times, our eyes can fool us; indeed, most of the time our five senses are in contrast to what God is saying. We need to know when to reason and when not to reason because the enemy knows the importance of obeying God. He can use these vulnerable moments, when we are in the valley of decision, to reason or talk us out of obedience and into disobedience through our senses. Before we know it, he has reasoned or talk us out of our blessings. Isaiah 1:18 says, "If ye be willing and obedient, ye shall eat the fat of the land." The question is, how do we know what the fat of the land is if we refuse to obey?

We cannot know what is on the other side if we fail to obey. There is a requirement for enjoying the abundance of God, or the fat of the land, and that requirement is to obey. Sometimes, the Creator tells us to forgive people, despite what they did to us, but our senses reason us out of doing it. We see things from our standpoint and so we find many reasons to not to forgive, and just like that, we are talked out of our blessings.

We need to guard our minds and be mindful of which voices we listen to. Philippians 4:7 says, "And the peace of God which transcends all understanding, will guard your hearts and minds in Christ Jesus."

The key word there is *guard*; the question is, what is to be guarded, and who is to guard it? The answer is right there—the mind and heart are to be guarded, and we are to guard them with the peace of God which surpasses or exceeds all understanding. All understanding include all human being and that of the enemy.

As I said earlier, certain decisions require deliberation while some require instant obedience. Let us examine reasoning as a tool for change, and let's look at Isaiah 1:18:

> Come now and let us reason together, saith the Lord;
> thou your sins be as scarlet, they shall white as snow;
> thou they be red like crimson, they shall be as wool.

Here, reasoning was initiated to change the mindset of the people. In other words, reasoning is an agent for change or the power to effect change. It should be clear that reasoning is an effective strategy to turn things around or to turn things in our favor. Reasoning has the potential to change an individual mind, and the enemy knows this; that is why he often tries to influence and manipulate us through his reasoning or conversation which is compounded with lies and deceit.

Look at how the enemy deceived Adam and Eve in the garden. The Creator said if they ate of the tree of knowledge of good and evil, they would surely die, but the enemy came in opposition to the Creator's word. He told Adam and Eve that if they ate of the tree of knowledge of good and evil, they surely would *not* die. He did not tell them a complete lie, but he mixed the lie with a piece of truth by telling them that their eyes would be opened, and this did happen. Half lie and half truth is still a lie.

> **PEOPLE WHO MANIPULATE OTHERS ATTACK THEIR MENTAL AND EMOTIONAL SIDES TO GET WHAT THEY WANT.**

Truth is truth. It is pure. It is not diluted with lies. From this lesson, we should conclude that we should not engaged in any civil conversation with the enemy except to use the word of God to rebut him when he says that we are not what God say we are. The enemy is a manipulator and he is also subtle. People who manipulate others attack their mental and emotional sides to get what they want. They take into consideration their tone, choice of words and the volume of knowledge that is needed to carry their attack. His main focus as we see above was to lured Adam and Eve into a conversation with him; moreover Eve who may tend to display more emotion than Adam, so that he can contradict what God says. He is a liar and a thief; he lied and he stole the spoken words of God from them. Be careful, the Enemy, is after the spoken words over your lives.

Having the facts and knowledge of the situation at hand is necessary when it comes to reasoning because you cannot reason above the knowledge you carry. More importantly, having the knowledge, consequences and solution for a situation available during reasoning is a bonus for convincing or persuading the listener. The enemy had knowledge of the tree and so he used that knowledge even though it was mixed with lies to convince Eve and Adam who had limited knowledge of the tree but refused to obey God whose knowledge exceeds them and that of the enemy. You have a greater probability of influencing someone's decision when you have thorough knowledge of the situation at hand. That is why you always should use reasoning as a strategy to change the minds of children who are heading for destruction.

Parents and older relatives, as the adults, have gone through different experiences and, in the process, have gained a wealth of knowledge. This knowledge and experience can be used to prevent children and others from making some of the mistakes and bad decisions the adults made. Based on the adults' vast knowledge and experiences, they can try to reason or talk children out of the impending destruction. Even though this strategy is very effective, the recipients have the final say because they have minds of their own. They can either choose to obey or disregard but their choices will determine the path ahead.

The enemy is always in contrast to what God is saying and as I said earlier, we have to shun his reasoning. That is what Adam and Eve failed to do. The enemy is an expert at trying to talk us out of our assignment with God. It is important that you know the mind of Christ and the mind that Christ has toward you. One way to know that is through his Word; study and meditate on it.

Remember that you cannot reason above the knowledge you carry. If you are not knowledgeable of who you are in the Creator, you will fall for the enemy's reasoning of who you are. When the enemy wants to reason you out of your purpose, among other things, speak the Word of God and shut him out. We can resist the enemy by speaking the truth over lies. Jesus resisted the enemy when he came to tempt him. The enemy had no other choice but to go. The more you apply the Word, the more he will flee. The thing is, you cannot apply what you don't have on the inside—you can't give what you don't have.

> **WE CAN RESIST THE ENEMY BY SPEAKING TRUTH OVER LIES**

It is imperative that our minds are guided in the right way—in accordance to the Creator's manual—so that we can reason or talk people into blessings rather than a curse. Isaiah 1:18 The Creator appealed through his prophet to bring the people together, to listen to them, and to tell them about their present state and the way forward. The aim of this was to divert them from the path they were on and to change their thinking.

God is the Creator, and he knows us better than we know ourselves. He came over as a father who was inviting his children to listen and take his advice. Remember that he is the supreme being. The word *supreme* means top or above; hence, his thinking is always above us. Here, the Creator is actually saying, "I have seen your wrongdoing and how profound and extreme it is." At the same time, he is saying, "It's not too late. I can help you. I can help you correct it and put you on the right path so that you can enjoy your best life."

The creator was asking to have a conversation with them even though he had a problem with the way they were living. His main intention was to fix the problem unlike the enemy whose intention is to create and escalate problems whenever we choose to engage with him.

He is actually saying that the best life comes when you and he reach a common ground. That is why he was implying " I want you to think about what I am saying". He was trying to bring their mind into agreement with his mind through dialogue and this was done with good intentions, that is, to forgive their sins and clean them up. Since his intentions toward you are good, the best decision you can make is to come into agreement with him. The Creator knows that change is up to us, but he still yearns for us to come into agreement with him to avoid any errors. The beauty of the Creator is that he has a track record of being right all of the time so it is always best to trust his judgment.

Looking at Isaiah 1:18–20, we can conclude that our minds have the ability to make us enjoy our best lives. They also have the potential to make us live our worst lives. Isaiah 1:19 clearly states, "If ye be willing and obedient, ye shall eat the good of the land." The words *willing* and *obedient* describe a mindset.

Your mind determines when to be obedient and when to be willing, so your mind needs to be renewed constantly. It will help you to discern right from wrong, according to the Creator's standards. When your mind is renewed, you will know when to obey or not obey as well as when to be willing or not willing. Your mind will be guided in the right direction.

We also see in Isaiah 1:18 that the Creator used reasoning as a form of reconciliation. We often see this strategy used in relationships, friendships, and family settings to bridge the gap. Here, we see that sin separated the children of Israel from the Creator and so reasoning was highlighted to bring them back to him. Even though their hearts and minds were far from him, which brought separation, he was willing to be reunited with them by bringing them into agreement with him. Their sinful lifestyle did not detour him from reaching out to reconcile with them. So the children of Israel had no reason to feel condemned because he [creator] knew the depths of their sin but was still willing to fix it.

THE TRANSITION OF POWER—TO BE IN CONTROL OF YOUR OWN MIND

When individuals give you responsibility, they are saying that they trust you to carry out the responsibility. Their expectation is that you will be loyal to the commitment, to carry out the responsibility.

Responsibilities often are given based on your ability and potential. The parable in Matthew 25:14–30 speaks of the three servants who were given responsibilities according to their talents and abilities. In that story, we see that success was inevitable because each individual was equipped with the necessary resources and abilities to carry out the responsibilities.

Let's look at our minds as our responsibilities. From the beginning of time, the Creator gave us the responsibility to take full control of our minds, and that comes with freedom of choice. This means we are free to make our own decisions. We are entitled to our own preferences and will, which means we are not robotic. Hence, we are not programmed by others to do what they want; we are free moral agents, able to think and make decisions for ourselves.

One of the first responsibilities that was given to man was to take care of the garden and to eat of the trees but *not* of the tree of knowledge of good and evil.

Adam and Eve did eat of the tree of knowledge of good and evil—it was freedom of choice. Here, we see their minds operating by their own choices instead of the Creator's choice. The Creator could have intervened, but he allowed Adam and Eve to be in control of their choices. The Creator said *don't*, but they felt that they should, as they had listened to another voice—the voice of the enemy. Here is a clear picture of the Creator allowing us to make our own decisions, despite his desiring us to obey what he says. The question now is, since the Creator has given us the responsibility to control our minds, what has he put in place so that we can think correctly, arrive at good decisions, and sustain righteous lifestyles? Two of the things he has given are his Word and the Holy Spirit.

> And be not conformed to this world: but be ye transformed by the renewing of your mind, that ye may prove what is that good and acceptable, will of God. (Romans 12:2)

Let's explore the scripture. The first part says we should not uphold or follow the standards of the world but should be changed by making over our minds and this could be done by implanting the Word of God in us so that we would be able to discern what is right or wrong, in keeping with the Creator's standards.

So one way to renew your mind is by studying and meditating on the Word of God—he made the mind and gave the remedy for positive and divine sustenance. In doing so, your mind will be transferred to the thinking of the Creator. The rationale here is that whatever you feed on will fuel or shape your future; that is, whatever you study, you will become. Whatever you feed on consumes you because it takes up residence in your mind and eventually your life. Whatever resides in your mind is reflected in your actions and behavior.

> **WHATEVER YOU FEED ON WILL FUEL OR SHAPE YOUR FUTURE.**

That is why it is essential to get rid of unwanted stuff that has been lodged and living in your mind over time. That is to get rid of that old mindset and old thinking, and replace it with a new mindset, which means a renewed mind. The Word of God will renew your mind because it is powerful and has life. Behind the Word of God is the Spirit of God—the Holy Spirit—who gives the Word life to clean out the impurities in our minds.

At this point, you can use the Word of God to train your mind to think divinely, positively, and correctly. Even though you have the power to make your own choices, whether bad or good, it will be different with a renewed mind because your mind will be guided to think divinely; that is, like the Creator. This will result in your making decisions that are in your best interest and the best interests of those around you. Most of all, it will be pleasing to the Creator. This is one reason why renewing the mind is so important for us. Becoming or living the Word is life-changing because the Word has life. It has the power to increase your life.

THE CREATOR'S INTENTION FOR MAN

> And God said, Let us make man in our image, after our likeness: and let them have dominion over the fish of the sea, and over the fowl of the air, and over every creeping thing that creepeth upon the earth. (Genesis 1:26)

When the Creator considered making man—humans—he thought about making man as a spirit being. Remember that God is a spirit, and it is the spirit of man that makes contact with God. Only a spirit can make contact with a spirit.

> God is a spirit: and they that worship him must worship him in spirit and in truth. (John 4:24)

Being spirit beings is what distinguishes us from animals. Animals cannot have fellowship with God because they are not spirit beings. Humans are spirit beings and so is God, and that is why humans were made to have fellowship and relationship with God.

God is a God of order, and he dealt with the spiritual aspect of humans first. Second, he thought about the human mind when he made reference to humans having dominion. The word *dominion* refers to a mindset; it has to do with our mentality. The mind has the power to rule, control, influence, and govern. Having dominion over things is having the power or authority to control things and not allow things to control you. Even before the Creator made humans, he gave us a synopsis of how the mind should function in relationship to things on earth—humans are spirit beings who have the power to control things and not allow things or people to control them. Many times, this is reversed; things control and dominate us while we are busy trying to dominate and control people around us.

When you carry the mind of the Creator, it means that you think like him; hence, there is no place for you to dominate people or to allow your life to be controlled by things. A renewed mind is vital because it shields you from being a victim to your thinking. We have many problems in society and in the body of Christ simply because we refuse to reestablish our minds according to the Creator's manual, which is the Word of God.

Remember that after the fall of man, sin entered man, and as a result, man's thinking became corrupt. In order for humans to think the way they were intended to think, a makeover is required. They need renewed minds, which means doing over their minds to their original or intended state—the state before the fall of man.

For example, if you purchase a car from Mitsubishi, you have to follow the manual from Mitsubishi on how to take care of your car. You cannot follow other automobile manuals, such as Corolla, Chrysler, or BMW, because those are not the manufacturer of your car. This is the problem humans have—they refuse to follow their maker's manuals;

instead, they seek help and listen to external voices, such as the enemy and some people around them who guide them poorly.

We can choose who can control our minds or after whom we should we pattern our minds. The thing is, no one knows the importance of an invention more than the inventor; no one knows the importance of a creation more than the creator. In the truest sense, if you are given the choice of who should control your mind, then the Creator would be the suitable choice, as he is the maker of it and has the knowledge to program it for success.

BE IN CONTROL OF YOUR THOUGHTS: IT CAN RUIN YOUR LIFE

I was lying on my bed when I began to think intently about my expenses, my plans, and what I had not achieved. I worried and then felt sad; I didn't want to get up from my bed, even though I needed to run a few errands. This feeling lasted for about half an hour. I then realized that this attitude was not conducive to a successful day. I had trained myself to shun negative, bad, evil, and pessimistic thoughts when they popped up because I knew that my actions—whether entertaining such thoughts or disregarding them—would determine the outcome of the situation. I immediately got up and said to myself, "I am a success story. I was created to fulfill a purpose, and my dreams are in view. I have an assignment to complete. I am a victor and not a victim, and my future is greater than my past and present."

What was I doing? I was taking my mind in the direction where I wanted it to go because I am in control of my thoughts. I realized that what consumes my mind will control my life. As soon as I began to redirect my mind to optimism, I felt the need to get things done.

> **THE MIND IS SO POWERFUL THAT YOUR BODY CANNOT GO WHERE THE MIND DOES NOT TAKE IT**

The mind is so powerful that your body cannot go where the mind does not take it. Our bodies are dependent on the mind to move; our bodies are subject to our mindsets. With that, I moved toward getting my errands done.

You can take back control of your mind by becoming aware and in sync with it. In doing so, you can achieve what you want. That is why it is important to train your mind to think divinely and positively. The mind is trainable; the more you train it with the Word of God, the more divine it will become; and it will be more useful, constructive, and positive.

As soon as I began to redirect my thoughts, my body began to move in the direction of getting things done. If the mind is in bondage, the body will remain in captivity.

Life is a reflection of how we think, and how we think will determine the path we take in life. In other words, our footsteps are guided by the level of our thinking and the mentality we uphold.

MY MIND BELIEVES ME

When I redirected my thinking, one word stood out: *believe*. The subconscious mind believes whatever you tell it. When I worried that my situation was too much and that I might not get past it, my mind believed it, and so my body came in alignment with my thinking. Afterward, there was a change in my mindset, and my mind believed that too—and my position changed. I got up and moved toward accomplishing my goals for the day.

Whatever you tell yourself, the mind accepts as the truth. When you see and hear things, the thoughts that come from these experiences determine what you believe.

Mark 4:24 says, "Take heed to what you hear." The thoughts that come after experiences likely will determine what you believe, and what you believe likely will come out in your behavior—and the way you act reinforces your belief. For example, if you frequently watch pornography, you develop thoughts of trying it because it looks pleasurable and satisfying. After trying, it might feel good to you, and so you may draw the conclusion that pornographic sex is the only sex that takes you to the highest climax and brings fulfillment. Now your belief becomes a part of your lifestyle.

Many of us would have met some people who want to get rid of certain behaviors, but find it very difficult and so they sometimes become frustrated and stuck in the process. Simply because their minds become corrupted because every time they indulge in bad practices, such as pornography practices, they are reinforcing the belief, and it becomes stronger and well seated in their subconscious minds.

This also happens when we repeat to ourselves, "I can't make it"; "I will always be poor"; or "My mother and sister died from cancer, so I will also die from cancer." Every time we think these thoughts, we reinforce the beliefs, and they become stronger and stronger until we accept them and believe them as the truth.

Remember that your subconscious mind will believes whatever you tell it. These beliefs will direct your behavior and feelings, which make them real to you, and you will have become what you say you are. After a while, you may realize that you are living a defeated life and that you need a change, only to find that changing your life is not as easy as you thought. So you keep going back, thinking and doing the same things, becoming stuck and frustrated. Long-held beliefs are made real over time; hence your mind will need reprograming—a new program. To acquire a new program, you'll need to make the old program obsolete.

> **LONG-HELD BELIEFS ARE MADE REAL OVER TIME**

THE SOLUTION

First, we need to give the Holy Spirit access to the subconscious mind. The Holy Spirit will identify the impurities and fix that which is corruptible with the Word of God. Then we can change the thoughts, feelings, and beliefs that are corrupting our thinking. This reprogramming is simply a renewal of the mind that gives the Holy Spirit access to our subconscious minds to stop the old, corrupted software from running and to add new programming (the Word of God), which is customized to our purposes and assignments. It is time that we reprogram our minds for success. Remember that our minds are like computers, and our thoughts and beliefs are like the software. We may not see them, but they are powerful enough to let us become them

TO WIN IS TO START BELIEVING IN YOURSELF

We need to wake our minds to the limitless possibilities that exist for us. I heard of a man whose career was abruptly brought to a halt when he suffered a spinal injury and was confined to a wheelchair. He was heartbroken because he had a family to take care of, but after leaving the hospital, he decided to readjust his thinking—to change it from "I can't" to "I can beat this tragedy." He prayed and asked the Creator to make him walk again, despite the doctors' diagnosis that he would not walk again. With that mindset, he got his wife involved, and the two of them began working toward his goal. At first, it seemed impossible and unachievable, but they never gave up on their belief; they were persistent. Eventually, one step at a time, he was able to walk on his own. His changed mindset and his confidence in the Creator were the key to his breakthrough; it removed the impossibilities in his life.

Believing in yourself is the first step to your victory. Your level of thinking pushes the Creator to work on your behalf. The reality is that God can only work with what we give him to work with. We must

> **WE MUST PARTICIPATE IN OUR VICTORY**

participate in our victory. Amos 3:3 says, "Can two walk together except they agree." The thing is, if you believe that you can't make it in life, and you walk around with the mentality of a loser, the Creator will be limited in performing on your behalf. The Creator cannot work unless you, the recipient of the victory, come into agreement with him so that he can give you the victory.

CHAPTER 2

SOUND KNOWLEDGE IS POWER

Sound knowledge or information accepted, interpreted, and executed is power and solution. As I get older, there are some things I had to unlearn to learn.

When I was a teenager, my teachers and other elders often told me that life is what you make it. These words seemed a cliché to me, but I was being a typical teenager who felt at that good things like success, achievements, and accomplishments would just happen to me. As I progressed in life, however, it became clearer to me that life could be a barren field, frozen with snow; life could be a broken-winged bird that cannot fly. These two metaphors were highlighted by the late poet Langston Hughes. From my point of view, I recognized that both the bird and the field have the ability to reach their potentials—that is, to fly and to be productive—but there are limitations. The field is unable to produce in winter, but that does not mean it cannot produce. When winter has passed and the snow has melted, that field will have the potential to produce because the limitation has been removed. That same field, however, could remain barren, even after the limitation is removed, if it's not given the required attention and nourishment.

Even though we may have setbacks, our lives should not be a reflection of failures and regrets but rather of our tenacity and perseverance, to stand in times of difficulties.

A broken-winged bird cannot fly; and that is a grim picture of life. Broken, however, does not mean death, so there is a measure of hope for the bird to fly again. This hope can come alive by accepting that there is damage and that it must be fixed. We can safely conclude that healing and change require awareness. Awareness means bringing yourself to the consciousness that there is something about you that needs fixing; awareness is being conscious of things that need to be changed or reformed. It is obvious, then, that awareness is vital for change and healing. In this case, to be fixed or healed is to fly again or to be made whole again.

Let us reflect on our lives in relation to Hughes's line, "Life could be a barren field, frozen with snow." Our lives are about seasons.

> And he shall be like a tree planted by the rivers of water, that bringeth forth his fruit in his season; his leaf also shall not whither; and whatsoever he doeth shall prosper. (Psalm 1:3)

Consider the words "in his season." This is an indication that we have our own seasons, or timing, and it is important that we know when it is our time to reap and when it is our time to sow. It is important to realize that when we are waiting on a particular season to pass, probably because of a bad experience, others are enjoying that same season because it is their time to shine and reap their rewards.

The barrenness can be termed as our waiting period. The field is not permanently barren; it was not producing at that time because of the cycles of nature. What the farmers do during this waiting period is critical; similarly, what we do during this period is also critical. Complaining should not be an option during this time; rather, we should prepare for the season that is to come, which will give us the liberty to produce. Seasons are temporary, and waiting actually means making preparations for what is to come and having the confidence and faith that our present season will be over soon.

What you do during your waiting period will determine your harvest. The ant in Proverbs 6:6–8 and Proverbs 30:25 gives us an idea of what we should do in our waiting period. The insects were diligently making preparation for the season to come. Success is predictable if we do what is necessary during our waiting season and that is to cultivate a positive minds, despite the challenges. This could be difficult at times and so that is why we need to train the mind to think positive at all times. In every season, it is important that we enter into it with a positive mindset in order to have a positive outcome. Here we are encouraged in scripture to keep a positive mindset.

> Finally, brethren, whatsoever things are honest, whatsoever things are just, whatsoever things are pure, whatsoever things are lovely, whatsoever things are of good report, if there be any virtue, and if there be any praise, think on these things. (Philippians 4:8)

The message here is to simply occupy your mind with these positive qualities. The positivity in our lives is as a result of our thinking because whatever we spend time thinking about will most surely grow and eventually consume us. When we choose to keep negative thoughts, we give them the energy necessary to fuel their growth.

There are some seasons when you have the control either to stay in it or take yourself out of it. Like the broken-winged bird, you either can fix the broken wing or leave it. When I was younger, I had to decide whether to wait on my dream job or occupy myself with other activities; I did the latter. I started a business with a relative and a friend; I made snacks, and they sold them for me. Instead of my becoming irritated during my waiting period, I decided to distract myself from the apprehensive mindset associated with prolonged waiting. Instead, I explored my hidden potential and occupied myself with a lot of reading. It was during this season that I rediscovered my hand skills and reactivated my passion for business, which to this day is a blessing for my life.

Our minds have the power to help us embrace and use every season meaningfully; as I've said, whatever we think about the most will grow and develop. If we choose to harbor negative thoughts, we give them the energy and nourishment they need to materialize.

Remember that limitations are temporary. Even though some of them are out of our control, like the snow on the field, they are still temporary. Success depends on what we do with our time when it is our waiting period. Our level of success is determined by the preparations we make while we wait. Reaching a place of wholeness is dependent on the preparations we make during our season of challenges, which is the season before our season of victory.

If life can be a barren field, then it also can be a productive field. In our quest for productivity, we must seek the appropriate knowledge to enable us to sustain productivity. Our thoughts must be in sync with the knowledge that is necessary for wholeness.

Knowledge consists of facts and information and skills. For us to acquire facts and information, we have to seek them. Knowledge is meant to be pursued, and if we are to be successful, we have to go after it. We must seek knowledge that will improve our lives in a positive way. This can include knowledge that will unlock the mysteries in our lives; knowledge that will guide us into our purposes and assignments here; knowledge that will help us to earn a living.

> **KNOWLEDGE IS MEANT TO BE PURSUED**

It is important to note that we were designed by the Creator to be productive, prosperous, and fertile. According to Pastor Leon Bogle, the mind functions based on the knowledge to which it is exposed. This means that we have the responsibility to equip ourselves with the information that is ideal for our development and success so that we each can unleash our potentials.

Being knowledgeable of what we have to do during our waiting period will determine the success of our harvest. The power is in our hands to either delay or reap success, based on our preparation, which is linked to the knowledge to which we are exposed.

When I was in high school, I disliked mathematics. In tenth grade, when my class was told to prepare for a math test, that was sad news for me—even emotional torture. I saw the teacher as an authority figure, being mentally abusive on a helpless child under the pretext of a math test; of course, my feelings were far from the truth. The day before the test, I reluctantly picked up my mathematics book to do a bit of practice. About twenty minutes later, l decided I was prepared, so I stopped studying and went to bed.

The following day in class, when I first glanced at the test paper, I thought, *Where do I begin?* Everything on the test paper seemed peculiar. I cowered in fear and felt reduced to the size of an ant. I counted every dirty spot on the wall and tried to figure out answers, but most of the time, I was unsuccessful. The truth is, I had not equipped myself with the knowledge I needed to be successful, so my mind could not rescue me by telling my brain what to do in that moment.

Research has shown that the mind works through the brain, and it is the mind that controls the brain. The brain responds from what you tell it to do, and what you tell it to do is your ability to think. Your ability to think effectively is based on the quality and volume of the knowledge to which you are exposed. In my case, my brain was unresponsive to the mathematics test because I was unable to think adequately on the subject, and that was due to my limited knowledge.

The Creator emphasizes the need for a renewed mind, and that means equipping the mind with the Word of God so that you will think in accordance of what the Word says. With a renewed mind, the Word of God reinforces the ability to think like him, which would then be reflected in your behavior and decision-making. The end result with my math test was that I was unsuccessful due to my having insufficient knowledge on the matter. Simply put, I could not apply what I did not know.

Hosea 4:6 declares, "My people are destroyed for the lack of knowledge." Here, we see the Word of God unfolding the truth that our lives can be ruined if we do not pursue the knowledge that is vital for our success.

Let's scrutinize the word *knowledge*. In Hebrew, the word means *light*, and light symbolizes awareness, understanding, clarity, and insight. On the contrary, *ignorance* means darkness, which is the opposite of light. Darkness symbolizes hatred, fear, and evil, for example. One way to maintain power over another person is by keeping that person in darkness. In other words, the oppressors control the

> **THE OPPRESSORS DISTRACT AND WITHHOLD THE TRUTH FROM THE OPPRESSED**

oppressed by way of darkness; by keeping them in ignorance. They take away the responsibility of knowing. The oppressors distract and withhold the truth from the oppressed, and they accomplish this goal by restricting their access to the knowledge, which is the light they need to guide them on a successful path. In doing so, the oppressed remain powerless because knowledge is power; it is meant to empower you.

The mind needs sound knowledge to empower it to make good decision. That is why only light is capable of getting rid of darkness. This is same as saying that knowledge is the solution for ignorance. If the oppressed remain in darkness or ignorance, they will never succeed or able to fulfill their purposes and become what they are intended to be.

The solution is liberation from darkness, and that is why light is the only solution for darkness—give knowledge and ignorance will disappear.

> **GIVE KNOWLEDGE AND IGNORANCE WILL DISAPPEAR**

Daniel 11:32 declares that the people who know their God shall be strong and do exploits. The question is, how do we know our God? We know our God through pursuing knowledge of him and using our minds to apply that knowledge effectively. The application of that knowledge will cause the believers to "do exploits"; that is, to achieve great things due to the effective use of that knowledge.

Oppressors know that very well, and that is why they try to control us by keeping us in darkness (ignorance), which is bondage, so that we will never be empowered to achieve anything great. They are quite aware that if they control our access to the right knowledge, then they are in control of us—remember that whoever controls the mind, the ability to think, controls us. The proper sustainability of the mind is dependent on the quality and volume of the knowledge it receives. Knowledge is food to the mind, and when applied effectively, it will improve our quality of life; this will be evident in our decisions, solutions, ideas, and imagination. The oppressors will always be in contrast to our mental development because they know it has the ability to drive us to the heights of success.

THE OPPRESSOR OF THE MIND

Our biggest oppressor of the mind in the spiritual realm is the enemy, the devil, Satan, Lucifer himself. He finds joy in interfering and meddling with our minds, the part within the brain that processes our thoughts, imagination, ideas, and words and that makes our decisions. He knows our minds are the embodiment of our lives and could be the epitome of our successes and failures.

Let's examine the first part of John 10:10—"The thief cometh not, but for to steal, and to kill, and to destroy." The thief, here, is the devil, who shows up to steal. One of the main things he is after is the Word of God in you and the Word of God spoken over you. He steals this through manipulation and lies. He is after the Word that is meant to empower you. Remember the Word of God, which is the knowledge of God, enfolds the mind of Christ and our success story. The enemy wants to steal it from us so that he can control us and deprive us of our success stories; it is the work of an oppressor.

Look what he did to Adam and Eve in the garden of Eden. The Creator gave Adam the word not to eat of the tree of knowledge of good and evil because if he did, he would die (Genesis 2: 17). Look what Satan, the oppressor, did; he stole the given word from the Creator from them and replaced it with his lies.

The enemy comes in various ways and styles because a professional thief does not always follow a definite pattern or trend. So as not to be caught, he uses different strategies to carry out his attack. Sometimes he roars to instill fear; sometimes he chuckles as he manipulates the mind; sometimes he screams to intimidate or terrify; sometimes he smiles to appear friendly; sometimes he whispers to soothe you. However he does it,

> **HE IS THE THIEF OF THE TRUTH, AND SO WITH EVERY LIE HE SAYS, TRUTH DIES WITHIN THE UNSTABLE AND VULNERABLE MINDS.**

his main purpose is to contradict or distort the truth—whatever the Word of God says. He is the thief of the truth, and so with every lie he says, truth dies within the unstable and vulnerable minds.

Always remember that words have life, and so when the enemy speaks, he is always ready to strike with his venom. His lies can cause injury or death as he tries to steal, destroy, and kill the truth, which is the Word of God. Knowing and standing firm in the truth will definitely prepare you for those attacks. You cannot win over your enemy if you do not know his strategies, weaknesses, and strengths. Knowledge is light, and this knowledge in fighting a battle is meant for guidance and direction. Light gives clarity, revelation, and enlightenment and is able to brighten a dark path by guiding you throughout your journey. If there is no light, you can be misled or stumble and fall.

Let's examine Psalm 119:105, which says, "Thy word is a lamp unto my feet and a light unto my path." In this scripture, the psalmist David is advocating that the knowledge or the Word of God, symbolized by the light, guides, directs, and pilots his life. He is confidently saying that his journey on the path called life is navigated by this light.

Light has the ability to illuminate; it gives revelation by disclosing, unearthing, and revealing things that were once a secret. In its truest sense, it has the ability to discover things and to reveal the unknown. It is important that we become aware of who we are by pursuing the knowledge that will reveal our true identities. Knowing who we are will facilitate effectiveness at our workplaces, churches, universities—in fact, any environment in which we are placed.

Natural things require natural insight or knowledge; physical things require physical insight or knowledge; spiritual things will require spiritual insight or knowledge. You can't be successful on a biology test if you study the Bible for that test. That would be absurd.

We are spiritual beings with human experiences. We require both the spiritual and natural knowledge to live a fulfilled life. In many instances, however, we are concerned only with the natural aspect of life.

WE ARE SPIRITUAL BEINGS WITH HUMAN EXPERIENCES.

First, we are spirit beings, and that is why a renewed mind is vital—a mind that is governed by the Word of God, which will help us to understand and bring clarity to things that the natural mind cannot comprehend. Until we become spiritual-minded and seek after spiritual things, we will never know certain things about ourselves because the natural mind cannot comprehend spiritual things—such things sound and look foolish to us.

In 1 Corinthians 2:14, Paul declared, "But the natural man receiveth not the things of the spirit of God; for they are foolish unto him: neither can he know them because they are spiritually discerned."

If we want to be more than conquerors and live a victorious life in Christ, we must seek the knowledge of the Holy Spirit and also study the Word of God diligently. According to Pastor Leon Bogle, it is the knowledge that you carry and its application that will determine your spirituality. You simply cannot function above the knowledge you carry.

Paul referred to the believers who were limited in knowledge as *babes in Christ*. For this reason, Paul encouraged the believers to take on the mind of Christ so that they could understand spiritual things. Here what he says in 1 Corinthians 2:12–13:

> Now we have received, not the spirit of the world, but the spirit, which is of God, that we may know the things freely given to us by God. Which things also we speak, not in the words which man's wisdom teacheth, but which the Holy Ghost; comparing spiritual things with spiritual.

That is why we should pursue spiritual knowledge because it has the ability to bring awareness, understanding, insight, and clarity to our lives.

On the other hand, we see why the devil wants to steal the light, which is the Word of God, from us. He simply knows it has the potential and power to transform our minds through the process of renewal. Renewing our minds means doing over our minds with the Word of God so that we will be able to think fully, like the Creator, in the way he intended for us to think from the beginning. Remember that a renewed mind is a do-over mind with the Word of God.

The mind can be renewed by studying the Word of God so that we will live it and also by being taught by the Holy Spirit, the greatest teacher, and anointed teachers, whether by reading books, watching television, or attending conferences, workshops, seminars, etc., so that we can grow in the knowledge and the light of the Word of God.

> And be not transformed to this world; but be ye transformed by the renewing of your mind, that ye may

prove what is that good, and acceptable will of God. (Romans 12:2)

Paul was admonishing the brethren to have their minds renewed because he knew the power of our minds on our behavior, decisions, feelings, emotions, and daily activities. Renewal of the mind is vital because the spiritual knowledge that we carry gives us the ability to think like Christ. We will be able to think beyond our natural ability. And the ability to think like Christ will give us the opportunity to prove that which is good and is the acceptable will of God for our lives.

Remember that we are spiritual beings who need spiritual guidance to live successful spiritual lives. This can be achieved through spiritual knowledge, with the Holy Spirit as our teacher, and a steadfast prayer life.

Having renewed minds does not mean that we will always make the right decisions. There are times when we probably will make bad choices; this is simply because we have the ability to think for ourselves. This is called freedom of choice. The fact is, it should be easier to correct our mistakes when we carry the mind of Christ because we are not wired to make choices against the will of God and also because of the active presence of the holy spirit in our lives but this is not always the case.

THE TRUTH ABOUT KNOWLEDGE IN GOD

In John 8:32, the Creator referred to his word as *truth*. He said, "And ye shall know the truth and the truth shall make you free." If you are living in ignorance or darkness, the truth, symbolized by light, is not in you. You are living in bondage because the purpose of the truth is to set you free. The truth has the power to bring awareness and liberate the mind, while ignorance has the power to contain or enclose the mind.

In Psalm 119:105, David describes the Word of God by saying, "Thy word is a lamp unto my feet and a light unto my path." Here, we see the Word of God being responsible for navigating our paths in this life, guiding our steps and course. Referred to as the light to our journey, it removes the darkness in our paths and takes us to our rightful destinations. Wherever we are and wherever we want to go, knowledge will take us there.

If there is a light on our paths, there also is a darkness on our paths, and if the Creator is responsible for the light—well, then, someone too is responsible for the darkness. Where there is good, evil always strives to compete. The intended purpose of evil is to keep us in darkness, while the intended purpose of the light is to bring clarity and show us the way to our destination in Christ. The enemy wants to keep us in darkness, but he can do so only to the degree of our ignorance. We can be controlled by the enemy for not knowing who we are in Christ. Not knowing (ignorance) paves the way for control and dominance by the enemy. One of the main purposes of knowing is to know who we are in Christ—that is our identity and the power and potential that lies within us.

KNOWLEDGE SOLVES PROBLEMS

Knowledge is the way of escape from ignorance; simply, knowledge is the cure for ignorance. For example, if you are driving and keep going in a circle, you cannot find your destination, and so you are stuck. Something is missing, and that something is the knowledge to find the destination. The only remedy is to be knowledgeable of what you are missing. Even if you decide to pray, you have to pray that you will receive the knowledge to find that destination.

Knowledge, both natural and spiritual, is meant to solve problems. For example, if you are a qualified dentist, your knowledge will solve my toothache. A gynecologist will deliver my baby safely. A prophet will prophesy over my life and tell me the reason for my failure.

> **KNOWLEDGE, BOTH NATURAL AND SPIRITUAL, IS MEANT TO SOLVE PROBLEMS**

The more knowledge you have in the Word of God, the more effective your prayer life will become. It is also important to note that the quality and volume of your knowledge and its application will determine your success. For example, if you are groomed by a sound and profound teacher in the field you are pursuing, whether secular or the heavenly kingdom, you will be on the road to success if you apply that knowledge, unlike being under tutelage of a lackadaisical, careless, or lazy teacher. A good teacher teaches his children to advance their lives. He or she makes learning possible by developing different strategies and methods to meet the needs of their children. In other words they study their children to find out what strategies will help their children to receive the knowledge they have to offer. Remember, the knowledge that the teacher carries is to help the students to solve their problems. All of us were created to solve a problem {our purpose] and so it takes the knowledge that is necessary to solve that problem. That is why we have anointed teachers that are available to help us solve our problems. The creator is the greatest teacher of all that will help us solve our problem, that is to fulfill our purpose. He has created us and he also created the knowledge to solve our problem.

I embrace these words: an investment in the right knowledge can only amount to a great return.

PURSUING KNOWLEDGE IS OUR RESPONSIBILITY

> My people are destroyed for lack of knowledge; because thou has rejected knowledge. (Hosea 4:6)

The people's lives were ruined. They put an end to their own lives by refusing to be informed or seeking the light, which was meant to set them free and give meaning to their life.

It is solely our responsibility to go after the knowledge necessary for our development, both physically and spiritually. We owe this to ourselves. We clearly see in Hosea 4:6 that knowledge in every aspect of our lives is a criterion for our existence. Without it and its application, we are powerless, hopeless, and purposeless. The latter part of Proverbs 11:9 declares, "but through knowledge shall the just be delivered." We can then conclude that ignorance is a threat to our success and deliverance.

Even though accessing the right knowledge is our responsibility, it is still

FAILURE IS PREDICTABLE WHEN WE REFUSE TO ACCESS KNOWLEDGE

a choice. In the scripture, we saw destruction as a choice, and this was based on the refusal to choose the right light, or knowledge. The scripture also shows that failure is predictable when we refused to access knowledge. Many people fail due to lack of knowledge, which leads to poor management.

You cannot manage effectively unless you are equipped with the knowledge to do so. One of the main reasons why people fail is because of lack of knowledge which leads to poor management. That is why the ability to manage your mind for success is based on the quality and volume of knowledge you feed it with. If you do not know the purpose for your existence, you will live your life below the expectation it is intended for (poor management), which is likely to lead to failure. On the other hand, if you are knowledgeable in your purpose, you have something worth living for and something to work toward. From this will come goals, objectives, plans, and full utilization of your time. Knowledge equips you with the power to do.

> And as such do wickedly against the covenant by flatteries: but the people that do know their God shall be strong, and do exploits. (Daniel 11:32)

Here we see that a requirement for being strong is to know and apply what you know. The word *exploit* means to make full use of. We are reminded to access and use the knowledge to the fullest extent for our advantage. It means, then, that the church should desire to know its God, and this will entail carrying the mind of Christ, to be equipped to destroy the enemy camp. Lack of the right knowledge is a criterion for failure and bad management. It is important that we sustain our minds with Word of God because the renewing of the mind is a continuous process. The more we train our minds with the Word of God, the more our minds will think wisely and take us to the height of success. Therefore, the sustainability of the mind is also dependent on how well we replenished it or how well we keep feeding it with the right knowledge. This is called management.

CHAPTER 3

THE BIGGEST THREAT TO MY PROSPERITY COULD BE ME

Sometimes your enemy is not your friends, family, or the devil but you.

Birds of a feather flock together—I can still hear this old proverb that my schoolteacher taught me as if it was yesterday. Repetition was one of the tool used to channel my mind and life in a specific direction. At that time, I knew that proverb had to do with grooming my life for the future. Later in life, I came to the realization that we become what we continuously hear, see, and practice. Whatever we continuously see and hear will get into our subconscious minds, and the end result is that we will become whatever we continuously see and hear. That is why it is important to associate with people whose habits and behavior can influence and impact our lives in a positive way.

The Creator reaffirmed this by declaring, "Iron sharpeneth iron; so a man sharpeneth the countenance of his friend" (Proverbs 27: 17). Basically, the choices we make in life can determine our destinies.

> **OUR ASSOCIATES COULD BE PITFALLS TO OUR SUCCESS**

As in the scripture, we see our associations should usher us into good things, such as our purposes, rather than diverting us into unprofitable lives. It is clear that our associates could be pitfalls to our success. We must shelter our lives from people who constantly try to debase us by labeling us as below our expectations and potentials. Persistent repetition of debasement can eventually turn our lives into disaster.

In Mark 4:23, the Creator says, "If any man have ears to hear, let them hear," but in Mark 4:24, he sheds more light by being specific: "Take heed to what you hear." It's not just that we have ears; we must listen and digest everything that people say to us. We must be selective in our hearing, and that means be careful of the voice we listen to because it has the power to either impact us or incapacitate us.

PITFALL ASSOCIATION

We can be enemies to our own success by associating with people who are a hindrance to their own success. People who find the time to gossip and are envious or jealous often procrastinate building their lives in a positive way. Associating with such people is too high a cost because you either become like them or fall prey to their behavior, thus prohibiting positive growth.

Some people never accept blame for their wrongdoing. Taking responsibility for your action is essential for change and healing, but these people are quick to see themselves as victims, and they walk around with the victim mentality. The enemy glories when we play the victim because he knows a solution cannot be reached until we accept our fault. That is, unless we accept that there is a problem, we cannot work toward a solution. Moreover, if we associate with people who seldom take responsibility for their actions, we may become the target that propels their victim mentality.

THE POWER OF CHOICE

One of our greatest responsibilities is to control what we allow into our minds. We have the power to train our minds however we want to train them, but it is the Creator's desire for us to train our minds according

> ONE OF OUR GREATEST RESPONSIBILITIES IS TO CONTROL WHAT WE ALLOW INTO OUR MINDS.

to his will. The Creator did not just give us this power and leave us on our own; he gave us the guidance and tools necessary so that it will be a blessings to us rather than an enemy. Remember that the Creator's intention is for us to study his Word so that we will take on the mind of Christ—to think like him so that our behavior and actions will reflect his thinking.

> For the word of God is quick, and powerful, and sharper than any two edged sword, piercing even to the dividing asunder of soul and spirit, and of the joints and marrow, and is a discerner of the thoughts and intents of the heart. (Hebrews 4:12)

Let me shed some light on the part of the scripture that says "and is a discerner of the thoughts." When we think, we build thoughts, and these become physical substances in our brains. In other words, it can creates images of what we are thinking. We begin to see what we are thinking, and it makes it more real. These thoughts are powerful—they are alive in our minds, and if we feed them, they will grow. And they can either be evil or good.

The Word of God in you, which is in keeping with a renewed mind, has the power and the ability to distinguished bad thoughts from good thoughts; that is, the thoughts that are meant to harm you from the ones that are meant to benefit you. The renewed mind is in place to stop the bad thoughts from growing and to enforce the Creator's desire for you in the situation.

When our minds are renewed, we will become in sync with it so that we can have control over our lives and basically achieve what we want. Our minds can be the deadliest or the friendliest things to us; it is a powerful force to reckon with, but it is trainable. If we feed our minds with the right food and exercise them, they definitely will develop into healthy minds. This is vital because our prosperity is based on a healthy mindset.

> **OUR MINDS CAN BE THE DEADLIEST OR THE FRIENDLIEST THINGS TO US.**

> Beloved, I wish above all things that thou mayest prosper and be in good health, even as thy soul prospereth. (3 John 2:2)

Here we see that for a prosperous life, prosperity must begin in our thinking. Above all things is better translated " in all aspects". John was actually telling Gaius that his mental health is important as his physical health. That is so true because you cannot prosper above the transformation of your mind. Which entails, you cannot change your physical health unless your mind says I will do so. Your ability to change you and your circumstances is determined by your thinking. I cannot change me until I change my thinking. According to Romans 12:2, If my mind is changed like unto the Creator I will know the perfect will of him for my life. What a spectacular place to be!

Consider the word *perfect*; this is above average. The word *perfect* means lacking nothing, completeness, wholeness. You will not lack the ability or potential to complete your assignment and purpose. The Creator emphasizes this fact in Philippians 2:5 by saying, "Let this mind be in you, which was also in Christ."

MAN, THE FALL, AND THE COMEBACK

Because of the fall of man in the book of Genesis, man's mind has drifted from the Creator's intended purpose. The Creator's solution to this problem, then, is have people do over their minds with the Word of God so that they can think like him again. This is to bring individuals back to God. People, however, are reluctant to accept that their minds need to be structured according to the Creator's manual; that is why our thinking has been detrimental to a prosperous lifestyle. People have become self-reliant, in the sense that they feel they don't need the Creator. They seek other knowledge that is incompatible to their development in the Creator. The minds that the Creator gave to us to do his will are now used to do things against his will, which is a disservice to ourselves and the Creator.

PUTTING THE CREATOR FIRST

The Word of God is God's manual for human life on earth because we need spiritual food to be effective in the spiritual realm. Not following the manual has driven people to think more about themselves and what they want to achieve, rather than fulfilling their purposes on earth. As a result of this thinking, people have gravitated more to the material things than the spiritual. Ponder on this: why are we more physical than spiritual when we are spirit beings, just living in a physical body? Because we are more inclined to take care of our physical needs instead of our spiritual needs.

> And God said unto him, because thou hast asked this thing, and hast not asked for thyself long life; neither hast asked for riches for thyself, nor hast asked the life of thine enemy; but hast asked for thyself understanding to discern judgement. Behold I have done according to thy words; lo, I have given thee a wise and an understanding heart; so that there was none like thee before thee, neither after thee shall any arise like unto thee. And I have given thee that which thou hast not asked, both riches and honour; so that there shall not be any among the kings like unto thee all thy days. And if thou wilt walk in my ways, to keep my statues and my commandments, as thy father David did walk then will I lengthen thy days. (1 Kings 3:11–14)

In the previous verse, we see the Creator asking Solomon what he wants. Solomon asks for an understanding heart to judge the people who are entrusted to his care. Fulfilling his God-given assignment was his first responsibility, and as a result, he asked for the wisdom that was necessary to fulfill that responsibility. It was evident that the Creator was Solomon's first priority because he put the Creator's interest above his own; consequently, he was rewarded with other things that he wanted.

The Creator, who is omniscient, knew that Solomon had a need for riches and wealth, and that is why he blessed Solomon with them.

We can be an enemy or a hindrance to our success by putting our own interests above the interest of God. Our mentality will determine whose interest we put first. We see in the scripture that when we look after the Creator's business, he will look after ours.

We should not neglect the creator's interests; we should prioritize. Many times, we work extremely hard to accomplish material things, and, in the process, we forget about our true purpose here on earth. I am not saying that we shouldn't work hard to accomplish certain materials things; no, I'm saying that some of us exhaust ourselves in trying to achieve these things. In the process, we lose our passion and zeal to pursue our purpose in God.

As you pursue your purpose, you will find that provision has been made for you to receive other things—the absolute truth is that there is provision in your purpose, and we see this clearly with Solomon, as well as with Abraham and Joseph, to name a few.

Abraham was about to kill his son Isaac, based on God's instruction. As he acted in obedience and was about to kill his son, an angel appeared and spoke to him and showed him the ram in the bushes. Here, we see provision in his purpose—a ram was provided—but the reality is that we do not experience the provision until we act accordingly and in obedience. This is putting God first and putting your faith to the test.

Hebrews 11:6 says that without faith, it is impossible to please, and living by faith is an act of obedience to the Creator. It is you saying, "God, I am not seeing any provision in this situation, but I know it is there, so I will act in obedience and faith."

> **LIVING BY FAITH IS AN ACT OF OBEDIENCE TO THE CREATOR**

Isaiah 1:19 declares, "If ye be willing and obedient, ye shall eat the good of the land." How would we know what is the good of the land, or how would we experience the good of the land if we don't act in faith and be obedient? We first have to believe what God says and then obey before we can experience that life. If we don't obey, how will we know what is on the other side? How will we experience that great life? Putting the creator first is an act of obedience to receive good things from the Lord.

OUR MINDSETS CAN EITHER SET US UP OR SET US DOWN

The mindset that we carry can push us to create a positive and favorable response from the Creator. Based on our choices, we can give God no other option but to bless us. Solomon's response pushed the Creator to bless him abundantly. The creator is bound to his word and principles; his reputation and his integrity is at stake. Hence when we do his will, he has no other option but to bless us for his name sake. On the contrary, your response can limit the hands of the Creator. Look at Matthew 13: 54 -58: speaks of Jesus when he went to his own country and taught the people in the synagogue ; they did not received him or his teachings and because of that he could not performed many miracles because of their unbelief.

Look at how the psalmist David describes the Creator's faithfulness to his word in Psalm 84:11: "For God is a sun and shield: the Lord will give grace and glory; no good thing will he uphold from them that walk uprightly."

Here, we see the Creator is bound by his word to bless us, as long as we walk uprightly. Psalm 23:3 says, "He restoreth my soul: he leadeth me in the paths of righteousness for his name's sake." The phrase *name's sake* means integrity's sake. Here again, we see that David put his trust in the Creator, and so the Creator was obligated to lead David into righteousness, for his integrity's and reputation's sake.

We may compromise our integrity for our own selfish gains, but the Creator doesn't operate like that because he is not like humans. He always keeps his word. He is the truth; hence, he has no other option but to perform to maintain his integrity and reputation.

Our actions can trigger an atmosphere for our healing, like the woman with the issue of blood. Our actions can trigger an atmosphere for wealth and riches, like Solomon. Our actions can trigger an atmosphere for protection, like David's protection from Saul. Our actions can trigger an atmosphere of blessings, like Joseph. We can cultivate a mindset that triggers favor and blessings from the Creator, instead of rejection and curses. Abel cultivated a reaction of blessings from God, while Cain cultivated a reaction of curses from the Creator. This means, therefore, that we have a choice and can trigger the atmosphere we want.

A PROSPEROUS MIND

> Beloved, I wish above all things that thou mayest prosper and be in good health, even as thy soul prospereth. (3 John 2:2)

Here, we see God places the mind as a number-one priority. It means that prosperity must first begin in the mind because if you are not prosperous in your mind, you will be a failure in every aspect of your life. The way you think will determine the prosperity of every aspect of your life; hence, the manifestation of a prosperous life is an evidence of your thinking. For you to live a prosperous life, you must uphold a prosperous mentality—remember that your thinking is a reflection of your life. Think first, and then the manifestation will follow. Prosperity is a mentality before it's a reality.

> **THE WAY YOU THINK WILL DETERMINE THE PROSPERITY OF EVERY ASPECT OF YOUR LIFE.**

Sadly, some people equate prosperity with wealth and riches. Riches are just a part of the definition. Prosperity includes good health, good relationships, peace of mind, good family relationships, and wealth. If being rich was the definition of prosperity, then affluent people would never be disgruntled, miserable, proud, or arrogant.

Let's look at the mindset of two rich men in the Bible. In Mark 10:17–27, the rich man asked Jesus what he must do to inherit eternal life. Jesus told the man to sell his riches and give the money to the poor. That was a very difficult thing to do, as the man had worked very hard to achieve what he had. When the Creator tells us to do something as big as that, however, it means something greater is already provided to replace it. How could we experience the greater blessings if we don't obey and act in faith?

Many of us have acquired material things and feel that we have attained the pinnacle of success. We didn't know that the Creator had so much more waiting for us, if only we had obeyed his instructions. This scenario played out in this rich man's life. He was rich, but his mind was not liberated to think beyond his riches.

Whatever we think about the most will grow and eventually

consume us. When we choose to put materials things first in our lives, we give them the attention and the energy to grow and consume us. The rich man walked away feeling sad because he was told to give away the thing that was first in his life, the thing that he loved dearly, and the thing that he thought about the most.

The story of the second rich man, Zacchaeus, is in Luke 19:1–10. Zacchaeus was a typical rich man but a rogue leader. As he listened to the Creator, he acted in obedience, which indicated his transformation. He first received the Creator, and then there was a transformation of his mind. His changed mindset was depicted when he decided to give to the poor and restore the things he had taken unlawfully; he did so without being prompted or told to do so.

A changed mindset is always reflected in our actions, behavior, and decisions, and this is what happened with Zacchaeus. His mind was already going through the renewal process. His response was in accordance to doing that which was good, accepted, and the perfect will of God. He thought in the way the Creator intended for him to think; he was mindful of others through obedience to God. A renewed mind breeds joy, happiness, contentment, peace, consideration, freedom, and love for others, and this was shown in Zacchaeus's response after an encounter with Jesus. As a result of his obedience and transformation, his entire family was saved. How much more important is our family than riches?

Zacchaeus was liberated from greed, covetousness, selfishness, and stealing. He and his household were saved and were happy, unlike the first rich man, who left the presence of God feeling sad because he chose to hold on to his riches.

We can be an enemy to our own success by holding on to things when we should let go of them to make way for greater things to come.

CHAPTER 4

BRINGING THE MIND INTO MATURITY.

Maturity is measured by your response during challenging times. The content of your mind—the way you think, choose, and feel—will produce your action during challenging times.

A lot of us like to consume foods that look appetizing, foods that tickle our taste buds and make our mouths water, but many times, the foods that look appetizing and tempting are not always good for us. Still, we eat them because they look good and taste great. Feasting on those foods, after a while, shows in our outer appearances, and there is a deterioration of our health or immune systems, with the possibility of death.

Eating to grow is a necessity, but eating to grow healthy is a choice. The potential to grow and live healthily is based on what we choose to eat; similarly, so is the mind. The mind has the potential to grow to maturity or to reach its full potential, based on the

> **EATING TO GROW IS A NECESSITY BUT EATING TO GROW HEALTHY IS A CHOICE.**

quality and volume of knowledge we feed it and to the degree that we apply that knowledge, which is our ability to think. Here, we see maturity is a choice, a self-development. To enforce this point, think of some people who have reached adulthood but their actions, behavior, and problem-solving or decision-making skills are childish and immature. Growing *old* is not a choice, but growing *up* is.

Our quality of life is vital to the fulfillment of our purposes. Let me shed some light on that statement. Genesis 35:29 tells us that Isaac died at the age of 180 years and that he was full of days when he died. David died at age seventy years, and when he died, it was said that he was full of days. When David died, he was 110 years younger than Isaac was at his death, but it was still mentioned that David was full of days when he died. *Full of days* is not a numerical statement but a qualitative statement, meaning how well the person lived his life; his quality of life. So "full of days" has nothing to do with quantity but with quality. A person could die at age twenty-five, having lived a life full of days, whereas a person who dies at age ninety might not fit that statement.

In the Bible, Methuselah was the oldest man who ever lived. He died at age 969 years, according to Genesis 5:27, but nothing was mentioned about the days he lived. A mature mind in Christ will reflect a quality life because it has the ability to think appropriately, effectively, and efficiently and to reflect or achieve a productive outcome. Our ability to think depicts the brilliance of the mind, and the brilliance of the mind is depicted by the application of the knowledge it receives. The mind will develop with consistent training and application of the knowledge it receives. It is so important that we manage our minds appropriately and divinely because our minds manage everything else about us.

AGE AND EXPERIENCE CAN BE A FACTOR FOR MATURITY

As we grow older, certain physical changes and growth take place internally, and these changes bring about maturity. The body matures and so does the mind as we grow toward adulthood. With age comes greater understanding, but there are many immature adults who have not yet grasped the essence of life. They lack that freedom to seek meaning beyond what they were taught or have read or experienced. Our physical growth must match our mental growth, which means that our physical and mental growth should be simultaneous so as to embrace maturity.

Maturity brings with it an independence to reason. Your reasoning carries weight based on the knowledge you carry. How can you reason with limited knowledge and expect to be effective?

People also mature based on experience and circumstances. David showed maturity through experience when he defeated Goliath. Let us examine this story in 1 Samuel 17:33-37. When Saul told David that he would not succeed against Goliath because he was inexperienced and young, David relied on his past experience to prove to Saul that he was fully ready, skillful, and capable of defeating Goliath. He told Saul that he had killed a lion and a bear without any assistance when they attacked his sheep. David was confident that the Creator who had enabled those victories would do the same for him with Goliath.

David's response to Saul was based on how he had reacted to his past circumstances. David's experiences gave him his personality and character. Whatever we learn and whatever we come to know molds us into that final person.

We must seek to know what is intended for us because what we know will take us out of certain circumstances.

FACTS ABOUT MATURITY

Maturity comes with accountability, responsibility, and capability. Many adult relationships suffer because there is lack of maturity; as a result, there is a lack of responsibility, accountability, capability, and understanding. There are a lot of failed relationships, not excluding a relationship with the Creator.

Immaturity is visible. Immature persons might be those whose spouses constantly beg them to treat them better, to refrain from putting them down, to listen and communicate with them, to not discuss their private business with their friends, and to be sensitive to their needs. The spouses would refer to them as children or as being immature because the spouses expect that, as adults, they should behave in a way that is consistent with maturity

Mature persons are distinguished from others based on the way they think. A leader

> **MATURE PERSONS ARE DISTINGUISHED FROM OTHERS BASED ON THE WAY THEY THINK.**

in the home, church, or workplace could never be a good leader without maturity because the characteristics of a good leader include building good relationships, knowing how to act in given situations, creating a peaceful environment, and knowing how to prioritize, solve problems, de-escalate, make proper decisions, and act appropriately in the face of chaos. These qualities are evident based on the way one thinks.

Maturity is a fruit of the mind, evidence of the knowledge you feed it. Acting maturely can stabilize a situation. The way we handle a situation could determine either a positive or negative outcome, and some decisions could haunt us for the rest of our lives.

Maturity is positive development, and it will be demonstrated in your service to humankind

TRAINING YIELDS SUCCESS

> But for solid food is for the matured, who by constant use have trained themselves to distinguished good from evil. (Hebrews 5:14)

The above scripture clearly highlights maturity as a choice that can be achieved by dedicated training to bring the mind in alignment with the Word of God. As we become older, our responsibility and accountability are greater, so it is important that we equip ourselves with the knowledge and the information that is relevant to the changes that come with the stages of life. Our level of maturity is tested by the application of the knowledge we possess; it's our ability to think. Constantly applying the right knowledge, such as the word of God, every day is the recipe for an upright lifestyle. Life is not about stagnancy and complacency but is more so about growth and development, which can come with experience and as a result maturity. For example, for an infant to develop into a toddler and the other childhood stages, he or she needs to be fed with the appropriate food at each stage of life to function in the capacity of his or her ability. This requires changes and adjustment in the diet at the various stages to accommodate the different developmental stages.

The scripture points out that maturity comes through constant training. One of the purposes of repetition is to perfect something, and in this case, it is by repeatedly feeding the mind with the Word of God and also executing it. Repeating this process has the power to control and bring the mind into submission to the will of God and to give one the ability to distinguish good from evil.

Training speaks of consistency, persistency, and commitment for a desired outcome. The mind, therefore, reflects the knowledge and the training it receives, which is sure to come out in our actions.

SOME PEOPLE ARE LIKE TREES—THEY TAKE FOREVER TO GROW UP

Immaturity is seen as a deficiency or a lack and is detected by the way you handle situations—the way you solve problems, the choices you make, your tolerance toward being corrected, etc. When there is lack, the ability to function effectively is compromised.

Some people never find the time to push their lives forward. They just sit around and accept whatever life throws at them. When they realize this—that they are stuck while the world is moving—regrets kick in, and they wish they were more proactive.

People should take full control of their lives by developing a mindset toward making things happen for themselves, instead of waiting for things to happen *to* them. We must take full control of our minds, which manage everything about us. The key word is *proactive*, which means that you are ready for something before it happens. We are born with potential and abilities that are waiting to be activated.

It takes awareness to value and understand the potential that lies within you. Bring the spotlight on the greatness inside you, and make the necessary changes to let that greatness become a reality. Failure to recognize your potential will prevent you from becoming what you were created to be.

Potential and maturity walk hand in hand. Your potential is waiting for your maturity to help bring it out and to sustain it.

Maturity is also understanding that how you manage your mind will determine the quality of your life. Again, maturity comes with accountability. You are accountable for molding, shaping, and training your mind by bringing it to the will and submission of God, so as to fulfill your purpose and assignment on earth. Submitting to the Creator's will is saying that his will is superior to your will. As you begin to mature there will be times when you will have to get rid of some things and take on something else in order to grow.

> When I was a child, I talked like a child, I thought like a child, I reasoned like a child. When I became a man I put away the ways of childhood. (1 Corinthians 13:1)

The above scripture acknowledges that growing into maturity means accepting that you have outlived your past, your childhood, and even your present experiences, and so it is time to move into your future and face another chapter in your life with confidence and assurance. Accepting that changes are vital for progress is the initial stage of getting something done. The change here is in accepting the responsibility that comes with aging by making the necessary changes in adulthood.

MATURITY, A WEAPON OF CONFIDENCE

Maturity doesn't save us from the complications of this world, but it helps us to understand them. Mature persons could remain peaceful while the world is in chaos, see possibilities while others see impossibilities, and act with confidence to get things done while others are in fear and panicking. In Ephesians 4:13-15, Paul tells the believers that until they become mature in the knowledge of God, they will continue to be like infants, tossed back and forth and carried about with every of doctrine.

> **MATURITY DOESN'T SAVE US FROM THE COMPLICATIONS OF THIS WORLD, BUT IT HELPS US TO UNDERSTAND THEM.**

Paul was saying that until you become built up in the knowledge of God, you will not understand what is going on in you and around you; hence, your attitude will reflect fear, anxiety, instability, and uncertainty. There was need for spiritual development.

When you are mature, you won't fall for everything that people say to you. Having a firm belief in something builds your confidence; it anchors you, especially if it is based on proven facts. It gives you hope when things seem hopeless. Paul told the believers to become mature in the knowledge of God so that they would not be deceived or become hopeless; rather they would be firmly grounded humans, to the measure of the stature of the fullness of Christ. We must be steadfast, unmovable, and unshakable in our belief in Christ.

James 1:18 concludes that a double-minded man is unstable in his ways. We must be firm by standing for something that is based on facts or from our own experience because if we are vulnerable, we can be persuaded to fall for anything that is said to us. And how do we get the facts? By seeking the knowledge or information that is relevant.

Those who don't stand for anything will give someone else the opportunity to think for them. This means they will open the door for people to impose their decisions, choices, feelings, and attitudes on them. It is not wrong to take advice, suggestions, or recommendations or even to ask someone to help you make a decision. The problem comes from setting a precedent, whereby someone always makes decisions and choices for you.

It is essential that we bring our minds to the place of maturity where we can think appropriately and ideally for the circumstances at hand. Let's not give people the right, power, and privilege to think for us. We are accountable for own lives, so it is our responsibility to exercise the power of thinking for ourselves—that was given to us by the Creator. Thinking for ourselves is a God-given ability; we are not robots that need to be programmed by someone who controls us. Our different choices are a reflection of our diverse thinking. In all of this, the Creator's desire is for us to align our minds with his Word so that our choices reflect his mindset.

CHAPTER 5

THE BATTLE FOR THE SOUL

Our fiercest battles are not fought on land, water, or air but in that place called the soul. That battle is real, and it is between good and evil.

Sometimes, one of the hardest things to do is to make a decision, and so we find ourselves stuck between a yes and a no.

In my high school years, I tried to figure out what I wanted to become. There were times when I wanted to be lawyer, a bank manager, a social worker—the list goes on. In the tenth grade, I pursued science. I was placed in the science class at that time; some of my very good friends were placed there too. Before long, however, I knew that was not what I wanted. I struggled to achieve good grades in that science class, my grades were always average or below. I barely passed and even failed once. My random choice of science created a limitation for my success—a truth I had to accept.

It was not until after I finished high school that I pursued becoming an English teacher. I had delayed my progress, however, and had to then take the subjects that would guarantee me entry into college to pursue my English career. The delay was a bit disappointing to me, but I did finally got an opportunity to pursue my English career before it was too late. Still, the delay could have been avoided if I had known what I wanted to become. Not being able to make important decisions in life can cause pain, frustration, and misery because you may find yourself living an unfulfilled or regrettable life.

One of the most uncomfortable positions is being in a job that does not fit your passion or desire. At the end of the day, you never feel accomplished or satisfied because as soon as you arrive at work, all you want to do is return home. You count the hours by the minute to get out of the workplace. When you are there, nothing makes much sense, and so you fret about the wasted hours, the wage, your duties, the environment, and so on.

Many of us started off at a job that we didn't like, but we knew it was going to be temporary because we were working on our dream plan simultaneously. Working on your dream plan gives you the energy and the motivation to diligently fulfill your temporary job because you know it's only for a short time and not a lifetime. One of the tragedies in life is wanting to *be* but not making preparation to be. We need to be our own facilitators of our change. That is making our change possible.

A MINDSET TOWARD CHANGE

Growth and change are inseparable. Changes comes with growth, and growth comes with changes. You change to become, and at the same time, you learn during your transformation process. Change takes place when we reach awareness, and that is at a point when the spotlight is shed on things that need to be changed so we can become what we want to become.

Changing for our betterment is vital to our prosperity and success in life, but growth and change for our betterment will also attract resistance because of the necessary sacrifices that we will have to make to facilitate that change. Many times, we have to abandon some things to accomplish the change for which we are looking. This requires bringing our minds to that place of change—a changed mindset. Our change begins in our minds and materializes in the outer world. Some of our habits, like procrastination, making excuses, or a lackadaisical approach to situations or circumstances, will have to go to make room for the replaced behavior that is in line

> **OUR CHANGE BEGINS IN OUR MINDS AND MATERIALIZES IN THE OUTER WORLD.**

with the changed mindset. Our old mindsets often are responsible for confining us to our present situations, so we need to take swift action to let go of the negatives that prevent our moving into the positive. This process can take time because some of these habits are due to constant practice. We have given these habits a lot of energy, which caused them to develop over the months or years, and now they are rooted firmly in us. When we gave our negative habits a lot of thought and attention, it is our responsibility then, to take back control of our lives by no longer giving them that energy, which will weaken them and diminish their growth so we can eventually get rid of them.

What You will be doing is taking away that power by weaning yourself off those negative habits that were built up over time; you will starve them of that energy by reprogramming your mind to do the opposite of those negative habits. For example, if you always procrastinate over doing important things, start putting dates and deadlines on your calendar for when you want to accomplished these things—and then work toward it. In doing this, you will reshape and reformulate your mind to accomplish the change you want to see.

Prayer is vital for change because God can direct, guide, and put new ideas in our thoughts concerning the change on which we are embarking. When we pray, it strengthens our faith and trust in God that we will be victorious in our change. Faith in God is vital. We are embarking on a changed mindset, so it means that our minds are involved; hence, there will be a struggle or a resistance because we are about to make a decision on where we are and where we want to go. A battle will ensue in the mind because there is a force—the enemy—who wants us to remain in the same situation where our lives are stagnating, while the Creator, wants us to make that change that will further progress us in life. It is at this juncture that many of us procrastinate and divert from our change. We listen to the enemy's voice, who often reasons us out of our change. We suddenly question our ability to be successful at such change, and we say we will do it later. Some of us may get confused and feel stuck between the two voices. One voice is saying we need to pursue the change; the other voice is saying no, not now, another time.

As we begin to think of making a decision, we are informed by the Creator and the enemy. This battle can be lost or won, based on our choice or preference, which is determined by that to which we give the most energy and attention. It is so important that our confidence is rooted in God so that we can shun all voices that go against his will and progress for our lives.

In any battle, there must be a winner and a loser. The question is, what part do you play in winning or losing your battle? The part you play is determined by to whom you give the power to rule your soul—to control your thinking, feelings, and choice.

THE PURSUIT OF THE SOUL

The soul is made up of the mind, which controls our thinking; our will, which controls our choices; and our emotions, which control our feelings. The mind is the center of the soul. The soul, in the Word of God, is used interchangeably with the mind, so it is the part of us where we think, feel, and choose.

There are two supernatural rulers of the soul, the devil and the Creator. Both of them want to be in control of your soul because both of them know that if they control your soul, they control you. This entails controlling your decisions, your behavior patterns, and your choices. The struggle that we encounter in our mind is as a result of those two supernatural beings contending to be in control—the fight is between good and evil. In this fight, good can only triumph over evil depending who you allow to rule your soul.

This battle never stops until you take your last breath on earth. Neither party is willing to let go because your soul matters. When the soul is in jeopardy, so is the family, the community, and the country because the soul of anything is the life of that thing. When we say we are fighting for the soul of our family, organization, or country, we are fighting for the life of it.

The devil's main intention is to hold your soul in captivity so that he can control you. Just as two physical armies fight to claim a territory, so does the enemy fight to claim the territory of your soul from the Creator. He pursues your soul to capture it, and when he does, he knows he has your life. You are now confined in his territory and restricted to his manipulative teaching. His teaching, of course, is contrary to the Creator's so he manipulates the truth to make the Creator looks like the liar. At this point, the truth is dying in you, and you are becoming the lie—remember that whatever you give energy to will grow and consume you. The big lie is meant to keep you in captivity and powerless, while the truth is meant to set you free. Your identity lies in the truth, and that is knowing who you are in Christ.

In addition, the truth is meant to empower you to become who you were created to be. The main reason the enemy is after your soul is to download the big lie into your subconscious mind so that you will become what he says you are. With this mindset, you will be a slave to the enemy, held in captivity of the mind; hence, you will be clueless, powerless, and unaware of who you are because you have been disarmed of the truth.

> Be sober, be vigilant; because your adversary, the devil as a roaring lion, walking about seeking whom he may devour. (1 Peter 5.8)

Here, we are reminded to keep a clear head—to think clearly, to be alert and awake—because the enemy is coming at us to either wipe us out or snatch the truth from us through perversion. He is out to devour our souls—take them over, engulf them, consume them, destroy them, ravage them. Remember that he is always in opposition to the truth. With every word he speaks, truth evaporates; truth dies.

The enemy brutally and savagely kills truth, and that is why his character is embodied in the following scripture, where he is seen as the father of lies, a manipulator, and a distorter of the truth:

> Ye are of your father, the devil and the lust of your father ye will do. He was a murderer from the beginning and abode not in the truth, because there is no truth in him. When he speaketh a lie, he speaketh of his own; for he is a liar and the father of it. (John 8:44)

We see clearly that the devil's intention is to devour the truth, so it is our responsibility to guard our souls where the battle is by seeking and holding on to the truth, which is the Word of God, the mind of Christ. Christ is the bearer of truth.

THE POWER OF THE MIND IN EVERYDAY LIFE

Just as the spirit needs a body to operate, so does the mind. The mind operates through the brain and the body. The mind tells the brain what to do; hence, the brain is only as small or large as the mind is, and it is only as intelligent as the mind is operating in its intelligence, according to science. The size of your brain is determined by the size of your mind. The question is, what is the size of your brain? Take into consideration that the brain is dependent on the mind to function at its optimum level. The mind is invisible, yet we see its manifestation through our daily agenda because the body works in sync with the mind.

As the mind makes the decision, the body carries it out. Consider this: the traffic light operates like the renewed mind. It makes the best decision to save lives on the road by telling you, the driver, when to stop, when to go, and when you should be cautious. But if the traffic light, which is a representation of a renewed mind, begins to malfunction because of a disconnection from its controller, which is the source of its power, there will be a lot of accidents, bad decisions, or bad judgment and chaos on the road. When it is time to stop, for example, the green light might come on, thus causing confusion and accidents. The malfunctioning traffic light is a representation of a chaotic mind, and a chaotic mind tends to make bad decisions that can interrupt the smooth flow of a day that was expected to go well.

We must stay connected to our source, the Creator, so that we will be inclined to do the right thing and make the right decisions. We are subject to malfunctioning if we disconnect from our source.

A THIN LINE BETWEEN RIGHT AND WRONG

Have you ever reached a traffic light as it's turning red, but a voice in your head tells you that no one is watching and there's no camera, so you should proceed instead of stopping? On the other hand, there is another voice telling you to stop and that the traffic rules should be obeyed at all times in order to avoid accidents and penalties.

You know what is right because the traffic light, your guide, is right ahead, telling you to stop, but you struggle to make the right decision because of that other voice that is urging you to make the wrong decision. Sometimes, we surrender and make the wrong choice because the enemy makes us feel that it is just a little thing. We don't realize that he is setting us up for this and other wrong behaviors to become a pattern.

We must be cognizant that being right is not debatable with the enemy because he is an expert in persuading us to cooperate with him to do the wrong thing. Since he is seeking our souls, it is essential that we consider carefully to whom we give the authority to rule our souls. The first place we lose the battle is in our thinking, and the decisions we make during these battles will determine the results.

THE MIND AT WORK

Our actions indicate that our minds are at work, and it gives others a clue of who is in control; the quality of our lives is determined by the quality of our mindsets. We are products of our own minds. Whatever we have sown into our minds will determine the fruits they give out; our actions will be determined by what we sow into our minds. A seed can only bring forth a fruit of its kind; likewise, our thinking can only bear the fruit of its kind. We cannot give out what is not inside us.

Look at Matthew 7:15–20. Verse 18 says, "A good tree cannot bring forth evil fruit neither can a corrupt tree bring forth good fruit," and verse 20 follows up by saying, "Wherefore by their fruits ye shall know them." People act from the character of their minds. Even if we can pretend for a while, the truth will come out because that is not who we really are. Who we are is based on the mindset we carry, and that mindset is based on the knowledge on which we feed and that we execute.

Success and prosperity are predictable in people—the way in which they use their minds is predictive of their success. When we look at some people, we are confident that they will be successful because their actions or works are a reminder of the way they think.

A seed can flourish into a tree only if it is planted in soil that is ideal for its growth and if it receives the necessities—sunlight, oxygen, and water. So it is with the mind. The Word of God, symbolized by the seed, can only fulfill its purpose if it is placed in the ideal soil, which is you. That is, the seed (Word of God) will grow in the soil (you), when the soil accepts the water (given by the Holy Spirit). This is to say that the mind can grow and develop in a positive way and make your life a success story if you accept the Word of God and allow the Holy Spirit to teach you to apply it in your everyday life. There is nothing wrong with the seed, but there are times when the seed is not placed in soil that is conducive to its growth. That is why Mark 4:4-8 talks about the results or the outcome when the seed is placed into the different types of soil.

THE BATTLE FOR THE SOUL

As long as we are alive, the intense battle for the soul never stops. It is continuous; it is a relentless pursuit because both the Creator and the enemy want to have rulership over our souls. The devil, the pursuer of the soul, will never give up on our souls because he always feels that he will claim our souls through his manipulation, lies, and deception. A continual prayer life and the application of the Word of God is vital for guarding our minds, bodies, and spirits from the lies and deception of the enemy.

THE ROLE OF THE SOUL DURING BATTLE

I was taught at school that humans are a higher class of animal, and this theory is backed by the animal rights movement (Ryder 1991), which says that humans are just animals with more intelligence. I was also taught in economics class that humans are economic animals that provide food, clothing, and shelter for their families. Evolution theory is that humans originated from ape-like ancestors.

Genesis 1:27 declares, "So God created man in his own image." We are created in the image of God, and God is considered a spirit being, according to John 4:24, which says, "God is a spirit and they that worship him must worship him in spirit and in truth." If we are made in the image and likeness of God, it means that we are spirit beings.

God made humans for fellowship and to have a relationship with him because they are in the same class and category. The Creator and humans cannot have fellowship with an animal because they are in a different kingdom; they are not spirit beings. We can conclude that humans are spirits who have souls and live in a body. The spirit, soul, and body are the three aspects of humans. The spirit deals with the spiritual things; it is the part of the individual that understands God. The soul deals with thinking (mind), feelings (emotions), and choice (will). The body deals with the physical aspect of humans. These three aspects each play a significant part in the continuous battle that goes on in our heads.

Remember that whatever decision your soul makes, your body carries it out, even if the spirit disagrees, because the mind, the center of the soul, is responsible for making the decisions in your life

Since the soul deals with our thinking, emotions, and feelings, the devil, who is the father of lies and manipulation, strives to manipulate our minds. He wants us to make decisions based on his thinking, which would definitely be contrary to our progress in life. The Creator wants us to carry out his will, but so does the enemy. The battle is so fierce because both parties want you to carry out their will and their purpose.

The enemy does his manipulation through lies, seduction, and subtlety. For example, as the truth is presented to you, he comes in and distorts that truth, intending to reason you away from the truth. He also lures you into looking at stuff that likely will entice or tease your emotions. As you look, it stimulates and arouses you, to the point that you want to feel what it is like, as with David and Bathsheba. All of this drama goes on in your mind. Your feelings, your emotions, and your thinking are put on trial, and you want to do the right thing, but there is a thirst to experience what you would have seen.

We need to pay heed to what we see and hear because that could be a stumbling block to our progress. To combat these battles, we must be aware of our identities—who we are in Christ and the power and authority that comes with that identity. We are liable to be overrun by the enemy if we don't take full control of our minds because he is very skillful at manipulation. He operates in different ways. As a predator eyeballs his prey, so does the enemy. Sometimes he waits in silence and creates an atmosphere of comfort. He entices his prey to come to his table; before long, he has taken you into his world. Sometimes, however, he comes with vengeance because has a short time to pour out his wrath.

> **AS A PREDATOR EYEBALLS HIS PREY, SO DOES THE ENEMY.**

Psalm 55:21 describes him like this: "The words of his mouth were smoother than butter, but war was in his heart: his words were softer than oil, yet were they drawn swords."

We can conclude that the enemy uses the mind as a port of entry to deceive and manipulate us. Sometimes we feel so overwhelmed, and that is because of the constant battle going on in our heads. Sometimes we become submerged in our thoughts and emotions, to the point that we become paralyzed in the middle of a situation. One voice is telling us to make one decision, and the other voice is telling us to make another decision—and we wander around in the valley of indecision. Many times, we want to make the right decision but we feel inclined to make the wrong decision; this attitude may be done out of persuasion or rebellion.

I was in situation where I was conscious that I was making the wrong choice, but I did it anyway. I made up my mind to do what I wanted to do because it felt and looked good, but later on, I regretted that decision. This is clearly the works of the flesh. There were other times when I knew the truth, but the devil manipulated the truth, and it sounds so good to me that I was driven to believe his lies. A trick of the enemy. I did not blame the devil for my action; I reconceptualized, rethinking and reviewing my actions. I could not change what had happened, but

I could prevent such mistake from reoccurring in the future. This was taking control of my future by correcting the past.

Many persons are guilty of knowing the truth but still becoming entrapped by the enemy's lies and making the wrong decisions. The tragedy in this is knowing what is right but choosing to do what is wrong. One of the ways we silence the flesh and the enemy is speaking to them from our place of authority [the word of God] and not from the place of our situation [that is what we see and hear]. The word empowers us to speak the mind of the Creator from the place of dominance and supremacy over the lies and the craving of the flesh. The word of God discerns our thoughts and also qualifies and certifies us to discard the ones that are detrimental to us. That is why a renewed mind is important, a mind that is consumed with the Word of God.

When the enemy tries to dilute the truth with his lies, remember that the Word of God is in you. It is the discerner of your thoughts and will inform you that the enemy's thought that shows itself is not good for you. One purpose of the Word is to discern your thoughts by identifying the bad thoughts and the good thoughts.

> For the word of God is quick, and powerful and sharper than any two edged sword, piercing even to the dividing asunder of soul and spirit, and of the joints and marrow, and is a discerner of the thoughts and intents of the heart. (Hebrews 4:12)

The discernment of thought is in keeping with a renewed mind, as in Romans 12:2: "that ye may prove what is that good, and acceptable, and perfect, will of God." After the thought has been discerned, you will know if you must keep it or discard it. If it is not of God, it is your responsibility to capture it and destroy it so that it will not become a reality; pull it down so it will not materialize.

What happens when an army captures its enemies? It brings them into captivity to destroy them—they are humiliated and have no way of escape; they are killed. Second Corinthians 10:5 tells us, "Casting down imaginations, and every high thing that exalteth itself against itself against the knowledge of God, and bringing into captivity every thought to the obedience of Christ."

It means that only godly thoughts should be lodged in your mind. Your mind should be renewed so that you are able to detect the godly thoughts. You will be unable to detect godly thoughts if the Word of God is not in you; a renewed mind that is empowered with the Word of God is able to discern and then destroy the thoughts from the enemy.

We can save ourselves from some of the pain we go through simply by being mindful of our thoughts, by becoming aware of the bad thoughts through discernment and then destroying them before they materialize and destroy us. The Creator did not just entrust our minds to our control, but he showed us how we can train and use our minds for our advantage. Some of the battles in our heads could be avoided if we allowed the Word of God to work in our minds.

We must be cognizant of our thought lives because thoughts are real; they are living; they are alive. When you feed them, giving them energy, they tend to grow. If you choose to keep a negative thought and give it energy, it will grow; whatever you think about the most will grow. Your negative thoughts will get bigger and bigger if you don't deal with them. They will be seen in your actions, behavior, and decision-making.

WHEN THEY ALL WORK TOGETHER

The spiritual, mental, and physical are the threefold nature of man. Let us see how they work. If we put them in order of rank, the spirit would be first, then the soul, and then the body. All of them are important because they have their different functions, so we should strive to bring all of them into alignment, with the Creator's standard. One of the benefits of having a Christlike spirit and a Christ-ruled body is that it aids the soul in making the right decisions and choices for our lives. The three working in harmony is important because change lies in the decision-making of our souls; the mindset we uphold will determine the choices we make.

Some people who have accepted Christ as their personal Savior still are involved in gossiping, lying, and even stealing and one of the reasons is simply because their minds have not been delivered from the old mindset and so there is no transformation in their minds. They still have the same old mindset. These people are stuck at accepting Christ. There is perhaps no follow-up of renewing their minds, which is supposed to be an ongoing process. That is why they continue to make bad choices.

For efficiency and productivity, we must pay attention to all three aspects of our lives, which means looking after the total person. Sometimes we can appear too spiritual and forget to attend to the physical needs of our brethren. James 2:15-16 tells us:

> If a brother or sister be naked, and destitute of daily food. And one of you say unto them, depart in peace, be ye warm and filled notwithstanding ye give them not those things which are needful to the body; what doth it profit?

On the other hand, we could become so caught up with the way we look physically that most of our time is spent on beautifying our bodies. In the process, we give little attention to our behavior pattern, our thinking, and the choices we make. This will create an imbalance in our lives that prevents us from functioning effectively and efficiently and having an impact. That is why Paul admonished the church at Thessalonica, "And the very God of peace sanctify you wholly, and I pray God your whole spirit and soul and body be preserved blamelessly unto the coming of our Lord Jesus Christ" (1 Thessalonians 5:23). Here, we see a glimpse that the threefold nature of humans is to be preserved, which means maintained in its entirety, without blame, at the coming of the Lord.

WHEN THE BATTLE IS IN PROCESS

We must be careful in what we indulge through our senses—that is, what we see, hear, touch, smell, and taste—because they can mislead us, with the help of the enemy. Adam and Eve in the garden were deceived through their senses. They listened when they should not have; she touched when she should not have; they tasted when they should not have.

When we spend time listening and looking at things that will not foster positive and spiritual growth, such as pornography, our bodies receive what the senses give to it; in this example, pornography would be seen and heard. The body then passes it to the spirit.

If your spirit is controlled by the Holy Spirit, it will immediately know if the information received is good or bad. If the spirit finds that the information is bad, it will tell the soul to tell the body to stop receiving that information—that is, to stop looking at pornography. Sometimes the body does not want to do what the spirit says and so will try to convince the soul by telling the soul that it loves what it saw and that it looks pleasurable and fulfilling.

The soul may tend to listen and ponders on what was said by the body, instead of dismissing it immediately. The more the soul ponders on what was said, the more it begins to feel emotionally aroused and stimulated, which drives it to decide that it can't pass up such an opportunity. In this case, the spirit has lost the battle because the mind made a decision that was in contrast to the spirit; now the spirit is occupied with worthless stuff. As the soul agrees with the body, the body now gets the green light from the soul to pursue that meaningless practice because the soul's decision worked in its favor.

Remember that the body is dependent on the soul to operate. When your soul receives information from the body, and you know that it is not good for you, it is essential that you dismiss it right away. You don't need to give energy to bad information, which will cause it to grow and become a reality. Lack of energy equals starvation and death. Plenty of energy equals growth and reality.

Every dimension of our lives must be balanced so that we can make good decisions. The spirit, soul, and body should be controlled by the Creator so they will be in agreement with each other when making decisions. In the situation above, we see the spirit was willing to make the right decision, but the soul and body were not willing to comply with the spirit. Also remember that behind all of this are the supernatural powers—good and evil—trying to prevail over each other. Even though sometimes all three dimensions of our lives are controlled by God—the

Holy Spirit is operating in our lives, our minds are renewed, and our bodies are presented as living sacrifices to the Creator—there is still a challenge sometimes to make the right decision because of the enemy's persistence to win over our souls. We must strive to be obedient to the Creator, despite the challenge, since his decision is best for our progress.

Luke 15:11–32 tells the story of the Prodigal Son. Verses 17 and 18 say, "When he came to his senses: he said, I am starving to death. I will set out and go to my father and say to him; father, I have sinned against heaven and against you." The statement "when he came to his senses" simply implies that when he began to think clearly, he got up and began the journey to his father's house. Here, we see the body responding to the right decision of the mind. Whether the mind makes the right or wrong decision, the body has to respond accordingly.

From time to time, the spirit gives the soul information to give to the body. If the Holy Spirit is active in us, our spirits will send righteous information to the body via the soul. Even though the spirit sends the information to the soul for the body to do, it is not guaranteed that the body will do it; the body can only act based on the decision of the soul. Whoever is ruling the soul at that time will determine the response from the soul. That is why we need the Holy Spirit be active in our lives—so that our spirits give righteous information to the soul, to give to the body, to then be carried out. Also, our souls should be renewed so that they will be happy and excited to have the body receive and accept the righteous information that was sent from the spirit.

A SCENE OF THE UNSEEN COURT ROOM

God—the supreme judge; assigns angels to fight his case
Devil—the accuser of the brethren; assigns demons to fight his case
Paul—a believer in Christ; determines who wins the battle

A car is left abandoned along a secluded roadside. Paul, who is a mechanic by trade, is walking along the same road to free himself from the noise and busyness of the town, when he discovers the car and decides to take a look.

THE MIND MATTERS

We will now look at the three dimensions of man (Paul) in operation.

Body: Oh! It's a green car, your favorite color. Wow! The seats are made with genuine leather. Touch it. Oh! This feels so good. It smells like Daisy, the Marc Jacobs cologne. I can't believe that I am sitting in a new Mercedes-Benz E-class sedan. Oh, soul! What do you think about this luxurious car? Oh my! Oh my!

Soul: I am getting so excited. I can't control my emotions. They are running wild. It has been a while since I've felt like this. Let me calm myself down—but this is truly unbelievable.

Spirit: Please tell Body to get out of the car. It is not his. Tell him to call the police and make a report about the abandoned car. The owner might be looking for his car. Be good, and tell him to do the right thing. If you don't make the right decision, there will be trouble.

Soul: I do not know what to do. I feel more like taking the car, but I might get into trouble, as Spirit said. I really want the car, but I am afraid of going to prison if I get caught. Let me tell Body what Spirit said.

Here, Paul is struggling with a decision about what to do. Body is trying to convince Soul to take the car, while Spirit is saying not to do it. Soul is stuck between the two decisions—one decision feels satisfying, pleasing and good; the other decision is right but it makes him feel dumb to pass up such an opportunity that rarely comes around. The reality is, one decision is right, and the other decision is wrong. Paul is aware that taking the car is wrong, but making the right decision is not always easy. The longer you ponder, the more difficult it becomes.

Body: But Soul, the color is so beautiful. I just googled it, and indeed, it is a new Mercedes Benz E-class. I see it is the most-recent model with a top speed of 174 mph, and it can gain momentum in just 4.1 seconds. It has a handcrafted 4.0 liter V8 biturbo engine with an EQ boost starter generator. I do not want to let it go. Please make up your mind and please yourself. I know you will not regret it.

Soul begins to contemplate on the exclusive features of the car, and now he sees himself driving that luxurious car. His imagination is taking a firm grip on him.

Spirit: Make Body get out of the car, and tell him to stop being misled by what he sees. Do not allow him to touch the car because it is not his car. Please; I am counting on you to make the right decision because if you make the wrong decision, it will come with consequences.

Soul: OK, Spirit. I know that what you are saying is right. I should not have entertained that conversation with Body. Oh my! Proverbs 20:17 is playing in my head: "Bread obtained by false hand is sweet to a man, but afterwards his mouth will be filled with gravel". I am not doing this anymore; it is just not right, and even though I am alone, the Creator is watching. I will not listen to Body anymore.

Body: Even though I really wanted to take it, I have to do what you say.

Body called the police and made a report about the abandoned car. If Soul had taken Body's advice, the outcome would have been different.

Paul made the right decision by listening to the voice of the Holy Spirit, even though it was challenging and also put the body under subjection; that is, to act in accordance of the Holy Spirit. As a result of Paul's decision, he was found not guilty of any wrongdoing by the supreme judge, the judge of all judges. Paul was not guilty because he acted within the confinement of the constitution (the Bible), the guide for life. The supreme judge is bound by the constitution, which is his own words, so he had to make his ruling based on that because he cannot override his word. His integrity and reputation are anchored in upholding the constitution. Ruling against it would have been a violation of the law and would have set a precedent for lawlessness, injustice and chaos.

If Paul had acted against the constitution—if he'd been disobedient—he would have had to face the penalty because disobedience comes with a penalty;

Evidently, there was a struggle within Paul to make the right decision, even though he knew right from wrong. Remember that your mind is like a courtroom, where good and evil are battling to win. The devil's intention—the accuser of the brethren, the father of lies—is never to lose a battle, while the Creator's intention—the defender of the brethren and truth—is to never give up on you and to be with you always.

Both parties want to win your soul, which is why the battle in the courtroom of the soul can become fierce sometimes. The enemy's intention is to kill the truth at any cost so as to keep his lies alive. On the other hand, the Creator's intention is to kill the lies so that truth can prevail. He is the truth, so the battle is based on keeping truth alive versus keeping lies alive.

> **THE ENEMY'S INTENTION IS TO KILL THE TRUTH AT ANY COST SO AS TO KEEP HIS LIES ALIVE.**

SEE THE DEVIL FOR WHO HE IS—MANIPULATOR, LIAR, DECEIVER, BETRAYER, TRAITOR

One of the enemy's goals is to bind you to his lies. We need to be conscious of the enemy's tactics because we can be enticed by his lies, which eventually could consume us. Before long, we will be spewing his lies. We automatically and unconsciously bind ourselves into a contract with the enemy to do his work or his will. The contract becomes legally binding when we carry out the agenda stipulated by the devil.

People often are unaware that they are legally binding themselves into a contract with the enemy when they choose to be continuously disobedient or act in contrast to what the Word of God says. For a contract to be binding, there must be an offer, acceptance, and performance. The devil is so subtle in that he binds you into contact with him without your knowledge. He does this by manipulation; he encourages you to act against the Creator's will. When you act against the Creator's will, you are carrying out the enemy's will. In this case, you accept his will not by saying it but by doing it. At this point, you are in a contract because the enemy offered it to you, and you accepted it because you are performing it. After a while, when you become tired of doing the enemy's will and you want to change, it can be very difficult because of the binding contract that you are not even aware of.

In the natural world, it is not easy to break a contract after you have bound yourself to an agreement with another person. Breaking contracts can end in disputes that must be settled in a court of law. In the spiritual realm, it is similar. The devil does not want to let go of you after you've entered into a contract with him; it is difficult to walk away. The devil will never allow you to leave his territory without a fight. Breaking a contract with the enemy is taken into the spiritual courtroom because demons were assigned to you to carry out the enemy's work, and they want to keep you bound. They can only be destroyed when they come into contact with the supernatural power of God.

The truth is, you gave the enemy the legal rights over your mind and life when you entered a contract with him, whether consciously or unconsciously. The enemy, therefore, had the legal right to your life; when you entered a contract with him, you bound yourself legally. In the spiritual courtroom, where the kingdom of light is headed by the supreme God, God is able to set you free from that binding contract with the kingdom of darkness. Since the contract was made legal in the spiritual realm, it will have to be nullified in the spiritual realm. The supreme God is always willing and ready to nullify these contracts, as long as you ask for forgiveness and seriously indicate to him that you want to be out of that contract with the enemy. That contract was formulated on lies, deception, and manipulation. Because the supreme God is a defender of the truth, he would therefore defend your cause.

Thanks be to the Creator that we can use prayers as a weapon in his spiritual courtroom against the devil, serving him an injunction to stop him from having control over our lives.

CHAPTER 6

THE TOXIC MINDSET

Guard your mind because toxic people are looking for a peaceful mind into which they will spew their toxic waste.

The toxic mind can be manipulative, judgmental, unapologetic, controlling, and self-centered. These negative descriptions are reflected in people, based on the way they think. These behavioral patterns can suck the joy and happiness out of your life simply because this group of people spend a lot of time on their own interests, and that destroys trust and respect and leads to superficial relationships with others.

The word *toxic* may be considered synonymous with bad, harmful, or dangerous. We should not expose ourselves to anything or anyone who is toxic because it is unhealthy, harmful, destructive, or poisonous and can be fatal. We avoid things that are labeled as toxic because they have the potential to harm us. Should we stay away from toxic people? Yes, we need to stay away from toxic people because the toxic waste that they give off has the potential to harm us, which could lead to spiritual death.

Self-preservation is a key factor in freeing ourselves from impending danger and in maintaining a healthy mind. Toxic substances can only harm us if they enter the body through inhalation, ingestion, or skin contact; when the body is exposed to that toxic substance. In the same way, our minds could become toxic when we take in the toxic waste that is discharged from the minds and through the mouths of toxic people.

Mark 4:24 says, "Take heed to what you hear." In other words, be careful to what you listen to because spoken words can either elevate or debase you spiritually, emotionally etc. Whatever you continuously listen to will eventually consume you. This is simply because you are giving it the energy and the attention it needs to grow—much like watering your plants so they will grow. If you continuously listen to the negative and judgmental words of toxic persons: before long, you will act in a toxic manner because the toxic waste of others will have found a port of entry, which is your mind, to download its contents, hence limiting your possibility to walk in your true potential.

Be careful of who you let into your inner circle. Staying away from toxic people does not mean you should stop talking to them. It means distancing yourself from conversations or practices that promote or give off toxic waste. Guard your mind by being deliberate and intentional in what you allow to take residence in your mind. You are in control of your mind, and you demonstrate this control by diverting yourself from any conversation or practice that is meant to harm you or those around you. A toxic mindset is very harmful because it messes with your mental health. For example, a relationship that is bad for your mental health would be described as toxic; likewise, a conversation that is bad for your mental health also would be described as toxic. You manage your mind by being accountable for what you let into and out of your mind. This is being mindful of your mind.

We need to be good stewards of our minds by utilizing and managing our minds properly—this is a priceless and precious gift that the creator has entrusted to our care. It is to be used for his glory

> **WE NEED TO BE GOOD STEWARDS OF OUR MINDS**

and honor and for the betterment of his creation. Managing our minds is our duty of care, and we need to manage them well because our minds manage our lives. Toxic behavior can be like a virus that spreads uncontained; like a cancer that destroys our lives and the lives of those around us. Toxic behavior is the result of a toxic mind, and a toxic mind is a result of toxic thoughts that have grown because they were given the energy necessary for growth. These same thoughts could have been destroyed by way of starvation—by not giving them the energy that stimulates their growth.

When we give energy to toxic thoughts, they will continue to grow and take up mental space in our minds. After a time, these thoughts likely will become our reality by manifesting in our actions, behavior, and conversation.

REMAINING TOXIC IS A CHOICE

Some of us become toxic because we were born into a toxic family; we were groomed and nurtured in that environment. Some of us become toxic because we were contaminated through association with toxic people. However we become toxic, we do not have to remain toxic. We have a Creator who has given us his Word, which is able to detox and renew our minds. We need to detox our minds from all of the harmful waste that does no good to us or those around us. It is slowly defeating our purposes and reducing us to the enemy's footstool. That is why it is necessary that we make the old mindset [toxic mindset] obsolete and replace it with the new mindset [transformed mindset]. The word of God consistently works and that is why we need to use it to our advantage. Detoxing and renewing is a continuous process, so we need to consistently feed on and apply the Word of God, which will drive out all of the toxic waste that develops in our thoughts, becoming habits that shape our lives.

In 2 Corinthians 10:5, Paul encouraged the believers to bring their thoughts into captivity to the obedience of Christ. In other words confined or constrained your thoughts to the obedience of God because If you do not capture those toxic thoughts, they will capture you and you will be restricted to the obedience of those toxic thoughts thus living a life below your abilities or expectations. These thoughts are distorted and can put your body into stress, which increases your vulnerability to illness.

Our bodies respond to our thought lives, and so we can choose to be either

> **OUR BODIES RESPOND TO OUR THOUGHT LIVES**

a victim or a victor of our thought lives. When we align our minds with the Word of God, our immune systems tend to function more effectively. One of the reason is that we are programmed for love because God is a God of love; we also are programmed for optimism. Our lives are designed to be confident and positive.

The apostle Paul's words to Timothy were, "For God hath not given us the spirit of fear; but of power, and of love, and of a sound mind" (2 Timothy 1:7).

We should have spirits of love and power and sound minds. When we act contrary to how we were designed, we are fearful instead of being courageous, we are hateful instead of loving and we have toxic minds instead of renewed minds; it means that we interrupt and change the structure of the way we were designed to function effectively. Changing our design works against God's intended purpose, and that can results in sickness, a toxic mindset, fearfulness, and weakness.

We should strive to be good stewards of our minds, which means managing our minds according to the Creator's standards so that our minds will operate in the fullness of their brilliance for the Creator's glory and for our gain.

THE CHANGE IS ME

We are created to be deeply intelligent and deeply intellectual. That is why we were entrusted with the responsibility of thinking and choosing for ourselves and making our own decisions. We are not robots; we can use our minds to think, which leads us to make choices. It is at this point of choosing that we can make bad decisions that can ruin our lives. Even though we are given the opportunity to choose, the Creator still desires for us to choose according to his Word. Our toxic mindset causes us to make some bad choices. How do we change our toxic mindsets in order to fulfill the Creator's purpose?

The first step to this change is self-discovery and self-awareness—recognizing that you are toxic.

The second step is working on detoxing, that is weaning or detaching yourself from the negative thoughts or thinking. The third step is replacing those negative thoughts with positive and Godly thoughts which is called transformation and this is mainly done by redoing your mind with the engrafted word, which is able to save your soul from further destruction. Whatever you plant in the network of your mind will influence the decisions that you make consciously. When you plant the word of truth in your soul or you continuously meditate on the Word, you are redesigning your mind to be like the Creator. That was its intended purpose, but it became distorted as a result of the fall of man in the garden.

James 1:21 declares, "Wherefore lay apart all filthiness and superfluity of naughtiness, and receive with meekness the engrafted word, which is able to save your souls." Here, we are reminded that the receiving of the Word into your soul is able to set you free from all toxicity.

The fourth step is maintenance. Maintaining a toxic-free mind means keeping connected to the source of your cleansing, who is the Creator. He keeps that which is committed unto him, according to 2 Timothy 1:12. That is why, in Philippians 4:7, Paul reminds the believers that the Creator is able to keep their minds and hearts in perfect peace. And in Philippians 4:8, he declares:

> Finally, brethren, whatsoever things are true, whatsoever things are honest, whatsoever things are just, whatsoever things are pure, whatsoever things are lovely, whatsoever things are of good report, if there be any virtue, and if there be any praise, think on these things.

This scripture reinforces that we are wired for love and positivity. Thinking contrary to that disrupts the purpose for a sound mind and a healthy and happy life. Thinking on good and positive qualities will drive out the hatred, envy, unforgiveness, worry, and anxiety. Having our minds always in tune with the Creator's standards is vital for maintenance. Living contrary to that, can create an opportunity for an unsound and toxic mind, which will put our bodies in a vulnerable state for sickness and diseases and suppress spiritual development.

The change is me; therefore, if my toxic mind needs to be fixed, it must start with me. Knowingly refusing to fix our minds is the same as accepting defeat.

IT ALWAYS BEGINS WITH A THOUGHT

Everything that came into existence firs began with a thought. What we say and what we do starts as thoughts in our heads. Thoughts proceed into words and then actions because we think, we say, and then we do.

The actions of a toxic person don't just happen; they begin with a thought. We must be mindful about our thoughts because our thoughts can ruin our lives, according to Charismatic Christian author Joyce Meyer. Acting on a thought can either progress or regress you because it has the potential to develop into reality. On the other hand, a thought can die or be killed due to rejection. Who has the power to kill or mature your thought? It is not the devil; it is not the creator; it is not others—it's you.

We were given that responsibility by the Creator, and so the power is in our hands to either develop or reject a thought. When we think, we are being enlightened by either God or the devil. The enemy can speak to us through the media or through friends or relatives, while Creator can speak to us through the Holy Spirit, prophets, and sermons. The choice is ours whether to listen to the Creator or the devil because that freedom was given to us by the Creator. That freedom gives us the responsibility to be in control of our thoughts. That is why it's important to be mindful of our thoughts.

Everything we perceive in the physical world has its origin in the unseen world of our thoughts and beliefs. Our thoughts create our reality; hence, they have the power to create the changes we want to manifest in our lives. Peace Pilgrim, a peace activist, has said, "If you realized how powerful your thoughts are, you would never think a negative thought."

Evil and toxic thoughts will pop up in our heads from time to time. It's our responsibility to take control of those thoughts by rejecting them. One way to do this is by redirecting our thinking to something that is good and pure. We are reminded in Philippians 4:8 to think on things that are honest, just, pure, and lovely. Likewise, in 2 Corinthians 10:5, we are reminded to bring our thoughts into captivity, which means to have control over them by restraining them so they have no power to materialize.

Because of our sinful nature and the enemy at work, we sometimes will have an urge to explore and do evil, especially if someone has done something to us that is ridiculous or wrong. When we descend into hell, however, we will have made a choice to ruin our lives because the toxic thoughts are fueled by dark forces that crave satisfying the flesh. That includes satisfying our own feelings. In such cases, we are likely to be victims of our own demise.

We are the masters of our heads and the guardians of our thoughts; hence, we can determine who or what we listen to and which information we download in our minds.

THE AUDACITY OF THE MIND

The mind is the most powerful and priceless gift from the Creator. The brain does intelligent things only when the mind is operating in its intelligence. It is my mind that causes me to make positive decisions and to use my ability for the betterment of myself and others. This same intelligent mind, however, can be described as a lethal weapon that has the propensity to turn or twist the truth to make it seems a lie, dreams into ashes, wealth into poverty, and peace into misery. The mind is not afraid to do good or evil, as long as we allow it.

We must manage our minds, which manages everything about us, in the right way. It is bold, courageous, and daring; it can make decisions, unapologetically, that can either progress us or ruin us. We are all managers because the Creator has given us the responsibility to manage our lives and things on earth. Managing our lives means managing our minds.

> **WE MUST MANAGE OUR MINDS, WHICH MANAGES EVERYTHING ABOUT US**

> Without counsel purposes are disappointed: but in the multitude of counselors they are established. (Proverbs 15:2)

The word *counsel* in the above scripture means guidance, information, instruction, advice. The scripture is saying that without guidance, our intended purpose is bound to fail. The purpose of our minds is to carry out the will of the Creator, but if we don't seek guidance on how to fulfill that purpose, that purpose will not become a reality.

For example, we all have a purpose to fulfill on earth, but just knowing our purpose is not enough. We must access and apply the information that is relevant to fulfill our purpose. We access this information through the Word of God, the Holy Spirit, and anointed men and women who are qualified. It is the same with our minds, which will only live out their purpose when we access the information necessary to carry out the will of God.

The mind and the will of the Creator is in his Word, but the scripture mentions that there are counselors whom the Creator has put in place to help elicit that purpose. These counselors include anointed men and women, such as teachers, pastors, or prophets, who are able to guide us to fulfill that purpose.

> That is why in Ephesians 4:11,12 declares, "So Christ himself gave apostles, prophets, evangelist, pastors and teachers to equip his people for work of service, so that the body of Christ may be built. (Ephesians 4:11–12)

These are the counselors who are assigned by the Creator to divinely guide us to fulfill purpose. A toxic mindset is a set back to enjoying life to its fullest and fulfilling your purpose in God.

A toxic mind cripples your vision to operate in your ability. You are either as small or as big as your mind is. We know that the mind is the enemy's main port of attack because when he gets our minds, he gets our lives.

> **YOU ARE EITHER AS SMALL OR AS BIG AS YOUR MIND IS.**

In our minds lies the power to *do* because when we think,

we usually make a choice or arrive at a decision. What I do and say is a result of what is going on in my mind, and what is going on in my mind will reflect the power to do good or evil.

Philippians 4:13 stimulates the mind to operate in its greatness and intelligence, as it tells us, "I can do all things through Christ which strengtheneth me." *I can do all things through Christ* is a mindset that will remove obstacles so you can reach to the peak of your potential. Restrictions and barriers should be used as stepping stones to reach the pinnacle of your life. A toxic mind is a dream- and destiny-killer; it stagnates growth. A renewed mind is a dream- and destiny-chaser. It saves your dreams and aspirations from dying.

James 1:21–22 encourages us to take in the Word of God and work it so that it saves our souls. Saving our souls is vital because when our souls are saved, the enemy is not in control. We will not only hear the Word but will apply it in every aspect of our lives. We will think success, prosper, be healthy, and have a positive impact and influence. These are the results of putting the Word to work in our lives. The active Word in our minds or lives and its application determines how big we are.

CHAPTER 7

THE CULTURED MINDSET

Are we more culture-driven or God-driven? Culture is very influential; hence, we must know how much is too much.

We may not be aware that we are rooted in our culture until we visit another environment with a different culture. We may then find it difficult to fit into another culture because adapting to change is not always easy. It can be one of the hardest things to do.

When I moved to Canada from Guyana, which is in the Caribbean, it was very difficult to fit into the Canadian culture; almost everything was different. The mode of dress was different due to the different weather conditions; the food was different; the accents and working environments were different. The lifestyle and community background were vastly different. I felt paralyzed and did not know how to begin my new life.

I thought I was mentally prepared for the changes, but when I got into the new environment, reality begin to unfold. I realized that I was not as prepared as I'd thought. I felt like returning to Guyana, but the thought of returning was too much to take in. I had to make an urgent decision to accept the changes and move on—and that was exactly what I did. I stopped dwelling on what I saw as different and focused on preparing my mind for the changes. I had to redesign my mind, and from then on, I made the necessary preparations for change.

Each of us is brought up and nourished in a particular culture, and so our minds are programmed to embrace and accept that culture. Our lives are modeled and shaped by our culture, including language, food, mode of dress, sports, music, and so on.

My first overseas trip was when I visited Suriname several years ago. I enjoyed my trip—the people were friendly, the food was great, and there were some beautiful sights. Yet I couldn't find restaurants that served the type of food that I was accustomed to, and I hoped to find a church where they sang my kind of music, with my kind of beat and rhythm. As I visited the beautiful sights, I kept hoping to meet someone who spoke like me, and of course I did. The country was beautiful; I had no complaints, but a part of me longed to be fulfilled. It was like a piece of me was still missing.

Our own culture can become so deeply rooted in us that it affects our enjoyment of other beautiful moments. Thinking about it can bring feelings of sadness, even when the environment promotes laugher and happiness.

Many believers' lives are in chaos because they come from one church with a certain mindset—they are accustomed to how things are done—and they go to another church with the expectation that other church should function in the same way. When they don't get that response, they either leave and do church-hopping to find that design they want, or they remain and become a problem by trying to fix things according to their customs or by finding fault in every person or the management.

Some churches are culture-driven instead of God-driven. The service is always planned in a particular way. Every Sunday, you have a good idea of what to expect. Planning is fine, but working without the Holy Spirit is nothing but a ritual. It's good to embrace culture, but when culture wants to interrupt our purpose in God, it should not be allowed.

> SOME CHURCHES ARE CULTURE-DRIVEN INSTEAD OF GOD-DRIVEN.

Even though we represent our culture, it must not define who we are. We represent a bigger picture and a bigger cause, and that is fulfilling the purpose we were created to fulfill. Our spiritual values should take precedence over our cultural values. The culture we embrace should not be a threat to our identity in Christ.

IDENTITY, PURPOSE, AND CULTURE

Identity, purpose, and culture can work hand in hand because we are made to embrace them, but if we do not put them in the correct order and prioritize them, we can be diverted from the Creator's intended plan for us.

You may be identified by your culture, but it is not your identity because your identity is who you are in Christ. For example, I am a child of God because I believe that he is my savior because he died on the cross for my sins, he paid my sins debt-something I possibly could not do for myself. This belief caused me to surrender my life to him. God created all things….so every person is a creature of God. But not every person is a child of God. God children are born of him too….but in a spiritual sense. God is my source because I came from him, and I can call him my Father. Your purpose is who you were created to be or why you exist, while your culture is the way you do things because of your associations and affiliations. Your purpose is personal because you are created with unique abilities to become what you were created to be. It is how you think uniquely to fulfill that purpose of becoming what you are destined to be.

Nobody else can fulfill that purpose like you do because of your unique and special way of thinking to fulfil that purpose. Your culture is not personal because you embrace practices that are shared by a group of people. You cannot change your God-given purpose, even though you may try, because your purpose is meant to be fulfilled by you. The Creator equipped you with the unique ability and capability to fulfill that purpose. You can change your culture, however, because culture is adaptable.

Your purpose is that engraved signature by the Creator that made you the ideal and unique person you are. Even though you may be walking contrary to fulfilling your purpose, your purpose never changes. Even if you decide to indulge in ungodly practices, God's plan and design for you never changes. You are only delaying the process by not being connected to the source of your purpose.

Everyone is connected to the Creator by their purpose because he created us with that unique purpose. It is only through him and by him that the purpose can be fulfilled, or it is only through him that we can be guided to become what we were created to be.

It is important what we are in right standing with the Creator and that we are in the right place, the right environment, so that the purpose of God can be fulfilled. Otherwise, we might find ourselves trying to fit into a particular culture that doesn't embrace or permit us to fulfill our purpose.

I have seen many persons abandon their purpose in an attempt to put culture over purpose. A lot of characters found themselves in this dilemma—Solomon, for example, in 1 Kings 11, who indulged in practices and beliefs that were forbidden by the Creator. The Creator told Solomon not to partake of those practices, but he abandoned his purpose to pursue ungodly practices. In Genesis 38, Judah moved away from his family, from under the covering of the Creator, and ventured into an environment that was not conducive to his fulfilling his purpose. The practices of that culture were forbidden by the Creator; hence, the aftermath.

WHEN CULTURE GETS IN THE WAY

Our culture is always a part of us; we take it with us wherever we go. We might immigrate to another country with a different culture, but we still practice our culture because that is what we have learned over time. Problems can arise when we allow our culture to consume our minds and we focus on that instead of living out our true identity and purpose.

Some people in the kingdom of God are more interested in governing the house of God based on their own practices and customs, rather than being led by the Spirit of God. These people, in most cases, are not open to change. They are stiff-necked in their ways. If there is a change in leadership, especially one who puts God first, these people find it difficult to flow with the new leadership, as a result of their conditioned mindsets. They are conditioned only to embrace their established culture in the house of God. You might hear some persons in the house of God lamenting about the good old days they used to have in the kingdom. They are frustrated and disappointed about where they are in the Lord and whose leadership they are under. They might complain that the current pastor doesn't do things like their former pastor did—the worship used to be more anointed—and that the believers used to be far more committed and dedicated. These excuses are sometimes because things go against the established plans in their heads.

It's not a problem to refer to past experiences under someone else's leadership, but this can become a problem if you allow the practices of your past environment to bring you to a standstill, where you can't see the possibilities that await you in the future. Gradually you will become a victim to your past environment and your established-culture mindset. You will be stuck, enslaved in your past, and probably won't even know it. You will be spiritually immobile, and it will become difficult for God to manifest himself through you because you will be focusing on where you used to be. Instead, you should focus on where you're going and who is guiding and directing you. You will live into the future with that mentality if you're not redirected to the Creator's guidance. That is a well established mindset that is detrimental to your progress.

This established-cultured mindset is a closed mindset, as it has no desire to open to changes; it's not willing to learn other perspectives. The open mindset is open to changes, open to the idea that there is much to learn. The renewed mind has an open mindset.

Mental success coach Ryan Gottfredson has described the differences between the open mindset (renewed mindset) and the closed mindset (culture mindset):

First, people with an open mindset always seek the truth, even if it means changing their minds, whereas those with a closed mindset seek to be right.

Second, those with an open mind are hungry to learn and to be guided; therefore, they seek others' perspectives, while those with a closed mindset have no desire to learn or seek others' perspectives.

Third, those with an open mindset recognize that while they may know a lot, they accept that there is much they don't know, while those with a closed mindset presume that they know enough.

Fourth, those with an open mindset are able to be objective about themselves and their knowledge, and they admit what they do not know. Those with a closed mindset are emotionally attached to their knowledge and have a hard time disconnecting from themselves; thus, they become defensive when challenged or given feedback.

CHANGE IS VITAL FOR PROGRESS

Change is unavoidable, if progress is to take place, but sometimes, it is not easy and can be very painful. When we decide to make a change, we are probably changing something that has become a habit, something that we are comfortable with, and this makes change one of the hardest things to do. It is going from a well-established way of doing something to a way that you will have to learn and practice. Even though it is difficult, it is attainable. It is bringing your mind to the place where you agree to uproot, dismantle, and redesign. This pain is definitely worthwhile because you will never experience the fullness of your potential until you make the necessary changes relevant to taking you there. You need an open mindset because that is a mind that is prepared to pursue the truth so that you can be guided into your assignment and purpose.

On the other hand, a closed mindset can be a hindrance to the truth, which is essential to liberate and set you free. One of the most difficult things to do is to transform from the closed mindset to the open mindset—from the culture mindset to a renewed mindset.

Some persons in the body of Christ carry the closed mindset, but it is important that these believers strive to move from the culture that some churches have set and to see the church as the body of Christ, which should be led by the Creator and is open to guidance and changes, as the Holy Spirit would direct. When you see the church as described above, it means that the believers under such a setting are moving ahead in the flow of the Creator and are not stagnated by the culture and set practices of an environment.

Avoid conforming to the set culture of some churches; rather, be conformed to the standards, precepts, rules, and principles of the Creator. In many churches, the Creator is not in charge of his own house, which is governed by the culture the people have set, with things being done their way. These churches have created a culture among the body of Christ, rather than an atmosphere. Some of the culture they created entails how many songs must be sung, how long the prayer should be, and sometimes even a recited prayer, a selected scripture, a chosen sermon, or a rigid dress code. Over time, after being groomed in that culture, you become accustomed to it, and it becomes a part of you. You begin to behave and act like everyone else who embraces that culture. That means that the Creator will be unable to function in that setting that has created a culture based on their preferences.

The Creator is likely to function in a church that is atmospheric because an atmosphere can be easily changed; it is not fixed or rigid and can be changed within seconds, either by a song, a prophetic word, a dance, a sermon, or perhaps a divine intervention.

Since the atmospheric church is open to changes, it is open to facilitating the Holy Spirit as its authority. The culture-mindset church tends to be rigid since they are groomed according to their own practices. The atmospheric-mindset church is dependent on change to function effectively, and change is dependent on a particular atmosphere to produce results. The atmospheric church is dependent on the Creator, who facilitates the necessary changes for his will to be done.

When persons with culture mindsets visit an atmospheric church, they encounter culture shock. It's difficult for them to fellowship under that setting because in their minds, they have built a culture of expectation of how all churches should be governed.

The Creator is bigger and greater than our culture, practices, and the norms of society. Culture can be a good thing because it can groom you to behave in a particular way that is necessary to fit into society, and the grooming can depict high moral standards. On the other hand, this influence can cause you to live in a box since it has the potential to confine an individual to its behavior, beliefs, and lifestyle. A mindset that stays on God will not allow the culture of a society to dictate its destiny.

CHAPTER 8

THE FEARS OF CONFRONTATION

Challenge fear by taking risk and doing the things that you feared the most. This act will surely bring an end to your fear.

During my school years, when the teacher asked a question, I would refuse to raise my hand to give the answer. This was simply because I was afraid of being wrong or what the other students might say, even though I often knew my answer was correct. I would not even try because the fear would consume me. Other times, I didn't understand what the teacher was teaching, but I would not say anything because I was so afraid. There was no penalty for not understanding, but still I was afraid. I sometimes failed a quiz because I hadn't told the teacher that I didn't understand. Living in fear will always amount to living below your expectations.

THE MIRROR, MY REFLECTIONS, AND MY FEARS

When we look into the mirror, we obviously see a reflection of ourselves. The mirror shows us the flaws, blemishes, defects, and imperfections that need to be fixed. Maybe your dress needs altering, your shirt collar needs adjusting, or your face needs a bit of moisturizing. When the mirror shows you the imperfection, it is your responsibility to decide whether or not you want to fix it. The choice is yours to ignore or correct the flaws and move on.

The Holy Spirit is like the mirror in our lives where we see ourselves through him. When we look to him for guidance, he reveals all of the impurities that are in our lives and all that we need to get rid of. The natural mirror, which I used as a representation of the Holy Spirit, is always right in its judgment. It never lies; it identifies flaws that we might have missed or couldn't see, and it's our responsibility to fix the fault or mistakes.

> **THE HOLY SPIRIT IS LIKE THE MIRROR IN OUR LIVES WHERE WE SEE OURSELVES THROUGH HIM**

If the fault is detected but is never fixed, the problem is not with the mirror but with your refusing to fix the fault. If a spouse or friend sees something amiss with your clothing or physical appearance, that person might ask, "Did you look at yourself in the mirror?" This question is asked because of the confidence they have in the mirror. We have confidence in the mirror because when we want to see if we look our best or close, the first thing we do is look in the mirror. The mirror justifies the perfection that we crave to achieve physically.

If we use the natural mirror to achieve our natural perfection, what are we using to achieve our spiritual perfection? The mirror here is the Holy Spirit.

The Holy Spirit is there to reveal things of which we are not knowledgeable. John 16:13 says, "Howbeit when he, the spirit of truth, is come, he will guide you into all truth." Just as the natural mirror reveals the truth, so does the Holy Spirit.

The natural or physical mirror can only work for natural perfection, and the Holy Spirit is for spiritual perfection. If we are spirit beings, we need the Holy Spirit to shed the spotlight on areas of our lives where we need improvement or change. Just as we cannot escape the natural mirror's showing us what we need to change or fix, so we need the Holy Spirit to highlight and bring awareness to what we need to change or improve to fulfill our purpose.

Some persons look into the natural mirror and recognize the flaws in their physical appearance but choose not to correct them. Similarly, when the Holy Spirit reveals to some believers what they need to change, they ignore the changes and try to continue with their normal lives—a decision that is detrimental to their progress in God. Sometimes they don't make changes because they are afraid to challenge their faults. It might require a process that exposes their faults, and so they may feel that it is better for them to conceal the faults rather than expose them, which might cause them shame. After a period of concealment, however, these faults become their biggest fears.

CONFRONTING YOUR FEARS

The only way to fight our fears is to confront them. Our fears can only be as deep as our minds allow. Some of us don't want to look into the mirror because we are afraid of what will be revealed to us—the enemy's trick. The reality is that we cannot destroy what we don't confront; we cannot fix what we don't challenge, and fear is one of those things.

> **OUR FEARS CAN ONLY BE AS DEEP AS OUR MINDS ALLOW.**

Sometimes, we don't want to look in the mirror because physical scars remind us of our history, and many times, it is a history that we don't want to remember. Many times, we try to hide that history with a mask or makeup. We try to erase those scars by repainting them, but they won't go anywhere until we deal with them. It's like putting fresh paint on a dilapidated house—the paint looks good externally, but it doesn't change the fact that the house will eventually crumble. The foundation, the core of the building, is shaky and was not given the attention needed to hold the structure firmly. It is only a matter of time before it finally collapses to the ground.

> **FEAR IS A STATE OF MIND**

Confronting our fears is a difficult thing to do because we might be confronting the wrongs we have done to other people. This might entail apologizing for deception and lies, which of course can be embarrassing and disappointing, especially if the persons have high expectations of you. Not wanting to confront these fears, however, brings torment. We are tormented by our fears because fear is a state of mind. It is a state of mind that is contrary to the state of mind the creator desires for his people. So when we operate out of fear, we are operating contrary to the mindset, the creator has designed for us. In 2 Timothy 1:7, "For God hath not given us the spirit of fear; but of power, and of love, and a sound mind.

Fear torments us because it is not a mindset we were designed to embrace. It torments us and makes us feel uncomfortable because it was not meant to be a part of us. It is a destiny killer. It opens the door to other demonic spirits. This spirit can take on many forms, but its intention is clear, no matter what kind of spirit of fear it maybe, it intends to keep you from fulfilling the assignment that the creator has on your life. It will take you from living a joyful, spirit led life to a life that is tormented by nightmares, that keeps you awake with little sleep. That is why Paul, the apostle, tells us to not be anxious for anything. Anxious is a form of fear.

Since our minds have not been programmed to harbor fear and negative emotions: then we should not desire to welcome or harbor fear in our lives. Let us examine this scripture 1John 4:18 " There is no fear in love; but perfect love casteth out fear: because fear hath torment. He that feareth is not made perfect in love". What is perfect love? Of course we know it to be Jesus, the one who died on the cross to set us free from these spirits and mindsets, but it is also him moving through us in love to other people. It is essential that we drive out fear, as the Creator has already paid the ransom for its release. He paid it with his death on the cross. Because the ransom has been paid in full, we are debt-free from fear, that tormenting mindset. It is our responsibility then to keep that freedom alive by walking in the mindset of a sound mind, the mindset he created us.

The enemy's plan is to keep us in bondage with an unsound mind which is considered to be an unhealthy mind, which could also be a fearful mind but the Creator's plan is for us to maintain the sound mind with which he created us, and in maintaining that mind, we must be able to confront our fears.

Confronting fear is a continuous process because the enemy always presents situations to instill fear in us, so as to divert us from reaching our goals and purpose in life. Fear is one of the enemy's attack on the mind to keep us in bondage. We must be willing to free ourselves from it, and one way we can free ourselves from fear and overcome it is by doing the things we are afraid to do.

Doing the things we are afraid to do is called courage. You never know how courageous you are until you stand up to fear, which will build your confidence. Eventually, that fear will die. Even though fear comes to defeat us, we can use that opportunity to show our true nature in Christ by confronting fear. We can challenge it by talking to ourselves positively and also reminding ourselves about what the word of God says about our strength in him and also praying to the Creator, who can empower and strengthen us. Talking to yourself positively and seeking the Creator's guidance reignites the power inside you to challenge your worst fear.

Look at the story of David in 1 Samuel 30:1–20. When death was looming over his head because the men wanted to stone him, it was a period of his worst fear, as well as the fear of losing his entire family, as they were in captivity. In verses 6 and 8, we see that David encouraged himself in the Lord and sought God's face. After doing so, David was strengthened and ready to take on his enemy.

When the enemy brings fear, use it to prove that you can be courageous in the midst of your adversity. If we allow fear to dominate our lives, it will defeat our purposes and plans that the Creator has for us because we would be fearful of launching and would not believe in ourselves. Many are in the grave with a book in their heads; many are in the grave with that medical invention. It is because they were afraid to try—probably because of that sinister voice that told them that they would never make it or that the idea would not work. That voice represents a dream-killer, a destiny-slayer and a purpose-assassin. That voice, sometimes, comes from within our inner circle, which can cause damaging effects because of the close connection the enemy uses to spew his false claims. The words of these false claims are alive and can therefore bear fruit and materialize, if not rejected forcefully. The words are also venomous because they are seasoned with hatred, malice, and envy.

WHY CONFRONT FEARS?

Because of the detrimental effects of fear and its hostility, we must confront it instead of approaching it. We do not approach fear because we know its intention and purpose—to keep us in bondage and to destroy our dreams and ambitions. When we approach, we do things in a calmer and gentler way, with the intention of inviting a conversation. This is definitely not a strategy for the enemy.

Instead, we must confront fear from the position of our authority—our position in Christ—and not from the standpoint of the situation. Otherwise, the situation will seem bigger than our authority. Our authority is the ability, power, and boldness with which the Creator has equipped us. Our intention in the situation must be to put fear to death, so we need to confront it with the mindset to conquer, destroy, resist, and challenge and in complete defiance of the enemy's pushing back. This is standing in solidarity with the Creator's mindset and standing from our position of authority.

> **WE MUST CONFRONT FEAR FROM THE POSITION OF OUR AUTHORITY**

A hostile environment needs aggression, standing up to the enemy and in noncompliance to him will yield results. When you want to kill anything, you act from the standpoint of your authority, and this is accompanied by aggressiveness, confidence, and boldness. Killing fear requires the same mentality.

Start looking at yourself in the mirror and speak to yourself: "I love you, and nothing will destroy or ruin you. You are not going to fall to pieces. You are not a failure or a victim but a success and a victor. You are more than a conqueror in Christ Jesus and you can do all things through Christ."

Put fear to death because living in fear is living a lie of who you really are. Fear always tells you that you can't do it. Fear defeats more people than any other thing in the world, as they are constantly tormented by their inability. Their inability always overshadows their capability. For these critical reasons, we need to sever ties with fear.

To live in fear is dying to your purpose, but to live by faith is the fulfilling of purpose. Fear is an enemy to our success while faith is a friend to our success.

Living in fear suffocates your true identity and purpose. It blocks the energy that is necessary for your potential and abilities to be developed and manifested. One of its intentions is to choke faith to death by not allowing it to breathe, taking away the hope we need to pursue life and fulfill our purpose in Christ.

> **FEAR IS AN ENEMY TO OUR SUCCESS WHILE FAITH IS A FRIEND TO OUR SUCCESS.**

Fear is of the devil, and it is in contrast to faith because without faith, it is impossible to please the Creator, according to Hebrews 11:6. If you are not pleasing the Creator, you are in disagreement with him. Amos 3:3 declares, "Can two walk together except they be agreed?" Let's reason this out: If the Creator created us with a unique purpose to be fulfilled, and we are in disagreement with him and not walking together with him, who will guide and direct us on fulfilling that purpose? Just think about it. Fear, which is of the enemy, is a threat to our potential because the Creator created us with potential; hence, he knows how we can work it to fulfill our purpose.

The enemy does not want us to fulfill our purpose; his intention is to keep us in fear. Living in fear involves dying, slowly and gradually, to your purpose because it is impossible to fulfill your purpose without faith in God. Faith entails living in God with great expectations to fulfill your purpose. When you have faith in the Creator, you will work those potentials and abilities without fear to accomplish your set goals, objectives, and plans—and, more so, his purpose.

Fear will come, but your response will determine the outcome of the situation.

We cannot control certain things that happen to us, but we can control our reactions to the situations. Our reactions are our choice, and our choice is either to choose life or death. Situations will always present themselves that drive fear into our lives, but how we respond to them will determine a victory or a defeat. Neuroscientists, such as Dr. Caroline Leaf, have concluded that many sicknesses or ailments are due to negative thoughts and fears. Our thinking activates certain genes. We don't have genes for cancer, alcoholism, or depression, but we have contorted and mutated things such as cancer and autism, for example, that come through our generations and can be manifested. They are sealed and under control, but they are unlocked by "the fear of manifesting these things." In other words, our fear will cause these genes to manifest these things in us. Being fearful stimulates these genes. Our choice to be fearful activates the genes to let these things manifest in our lives.

We also have a choice not to give in to fear. We have a choice to declare that these things will not be our portion; they will not be our destiny.

It is important to have your annual checkups, but the problem will be if you go with the fear that the doctor will give you that bad news. Don't forget that your thinking can activates the genes for sicknesses, so it's important to get rid of fear so as not to activate the genes for those ailments. This is one of the strategies that the enemy uses to make us feel like victims. He wants to keep us in fear.

Society also helps to keep us in fear because when society sees that your parents or perhaps your sibling are suffering with cancer, autism, depression, or ADHD, they will tell you that you have a gene for those things. We cannot control what people might say to us because they are talking based on their mindset, but how we respond to that is our choice that can determine the outcome.

What about the children who were born with autism or Down syndrome, something that they did not choose. It is important that we do not react by blaming God for bringing this on the individual. This reaction will worsen the situation. These disorders have manifested as a result of changes that came through Adam and Eve's bloodline, which they manifested. This is a result of the fall of man with the introduction of sin. How we react in these situations can cause the Creator to change the situation or we can choose to look beyond the limitations of those individuals and capitalize on their strengths and the beauty and fulfillment those individuals add to the relationship.

HUMANS' GREATEST FEARS

Let us look at humans' greatest fear, from the standpoint of Job's misfortunes.

> For the thing which I greatly feared is come upon me, and
> that which I was afraid of is come unto me. (Job 3:25)

Job was an upright man, and according to Job 1, he eschewed evil. Even though he was upright, he was a bit fearful, he was a bit concerned if ever he would have to face losing those things as we all did at some point of our lives. In Job 3:25, he confessed that the thing that he greatly feared had come upon him. The Creator knew Job thought of being fearful and at the same he knew Job faith was grounded in him. The creator tested him on the same thing that he was fearful of losing—his family, his livestock, and his health. The fear of losing these things happened to him. God has a way of testing us with the things we love dearly, to see our response; if we love these people or things more than him.

Men's worst fears are of losing their loved ones, especially those who are closest to their hearts; their possessions that are very dear to them; and their health, which is their physical strength. The Creator knew that even though Job was fearful of losing these things, he would not bow under any circumstances, and that is why he boasted of him to the enemy.

The thing we fear is the same thing that, most times, happens to us, and it has the potential to bring us down. Job was able to make a great comeback, and it was all because of his response to the situation.

On the other hand look at Abraham's response when he was asked to kill his only son as a sacrifice. Abraham obeyed immediately, without being fearful of losing his son. He was tested on his obedience, and he came out victorious because of his response. As a result, he was blessed tremendously, and in his seed, all the nations of the earth are blessed. If he had responded differently, the outcome would have been different.

In Job's case, he could have responded to his wife's request to curse God and die (Job 2:9), but he bluntly refused such a suggestion and stayed with the Creator, despite the situation. The outcome would have been different if he had chosen death, as his wife suggested. Because of Job's reaction to the situation, the Lord restored him bountifully, and he was given twice as much as he had before (Job 42:10–17).

> And the Lord blessed the latter days of Job more than his beginning, for he had 14,000 sheep, 6000 camels, 1000 yoke of oxen and 1000 female donkeys. (Job 42:12)

He had seven sons and three daughters, and in all the land, there were found no women as fair as the daughters of Job (Job 42:15). Job lived 140 years and saw his sons and his grandson, four generations (Job 42:16). Job died an old man and full of days (Job 42:17).

All of this was a result of Job's reaction to the situation. He chose not to be a victim but a victor in progress. He chose not to give in, although it was a scary situation, but to stand tall and still trust the Creator, when those closest to him told him otherwise.

Can the creator boast about us? Are we willing to choose faith instead of fear?

You may become fearful in a situation, but don't let fear become your permanent mindset. Henry Ford once said, "One of the greatest discoveries a man makes, one of his great surprises, is to find he can do what he was afraid he couldn't do."

The Creator's desire is to bring us to the point where we see ourselves as sojourners, where we are just passing through here on earth, only for a time. Everything we have here is loaned to us, whether it is our children, properties, livestock, or bank account. When we die, we leave it all behind.

> And Job said naked came I out of my mother womb and naked shall I return thither; the Lord gave and the Lord had taken away; blessed be the name of the Lord. (Job 1:21)

I must admit that it is difficult sometimes to bring your mind to think like this, but building a close relationship with the Creator through constant prayer and fasting, meditating, applying the Word of God, and having a mindset of an overcomer will definitely defeat the mindset of fear. You may begin this journey being fearful, but you don't have to end it being fearful. Some of us continue to be fearful to the end, and we die in fear. A comeback is necessary for a victory.

Job was fearful of losing those things but he responded to his fears with faith even though there were times when it was really challenging and it was heard in his cries. When we look at the woman with the issue of blood, she was not willing to give up, despite her situation. Faith brought hope to the situation, and she responded with that mindset to overcome the fear of death. Just as fear activates the genes to unlock sicknesses, we can use faith to unlock our potentials and to keep those genes shut so they never harm us.

CHAPTER 9

THE MIND OF CHRIST TOWARD YOU

For I know the thoughts that I think towards you, saith the Lord, thoughts of peace and not of evil, to give you an expected end.
—Jeremiah 29:11

The Creator's thoughts toward us are pure and authentic, and he expects us to end our race well. The way we think of others determines how we treat or react to them. Here, we see that because the Creator's thoughts toward us are good, he wants to give us a good future. Our thoughts toward people can be good or bad, and based on those thoughts, we will have either positive or negative feelings toward them. The critical thing here is that sometimes our thoughts can mislead us and cause us to think wrongly toward a person.

The Creator says in Jeremiah 29:11, "I know the thoughts I think towards you." He is fully confident in his thoughts toward us. The Creator is well aware and conscious of his thoughts, and so it is also important that we be in sync with our thoughts toward each other. To know your thoughts is to become aware of what you are thinking or having an insight of what you are thinking.

When the Creator said that he "knows the thought that he think towards us," it means that he is well aware that he wants the best for us. Being aware of or in tune with your thoughts will enable you to separate the bad thoughts from the good thoughts; to discard the bad thoughts and keep the good thoughts.

Hebrews 4:12 declares that the Word of God is a discerner of the thoughts, which means the Word of God, which is alive and active, is able to expose the bad thoughts and judge whether our thoughts are good or bad. The holy spirit, the spirit of truth, also determines which thoughts we need to get rid of.

Many times, we don't only have bad thoughts about other people but also bad thoughts about ourselves, which could be detrimental to our well-being. These negative thoughts are mostly amplified by the enemy. The enemy knows that our thoughts are a catalyst for self-perpetuating cycles. If you think you are a loser, you will feel like a loser. Then you will act like a loser. This assumption leads to discouragement and causes you to want to stop trying and, ultimately, to give up.

Psychologist Amy Morin explains that "once you draw a conclusion about yourself, you are likely to do two things: (1) look for evidence that reinforces your beliefs, and (2) discount anything that runs contrary to your belief." A person who develops the belief that he is a loser, for example, will view each mistake as his not being good enough. When such person does not succeed at something, he probably will say that he knew that would be the outcome.

So many times, the way we think keeps us from reaching our full potential. The truth, not because we think something, makes it true. Having a renewed mind is very important because it will challenge those negative beliefs about ourselves. A renewed mind gives us a positive outlook on life, which leads to optimistic thoughts, productive behavior, and, eventually, a successful outcome. Most of the time, it is not our lack of talent or skills that holds us back. Instead, many times, it is the way we think, which enforces the way we see ourselves and keeps us from performing at our peak. Seeing ourselves through the mind of the Creator can lead to a better and more productive outcome.

Everything the Creator says about you, the enemy opposes. The enemy is always in opposition to the truth. That is why the enemy was cast out from the presence of the Creator, from heaven, simply because he wanted to oppose God and be God.

See yourself through the mind of the Creator, as one who is beautifully and fearfully made and blessed with talents, skills, and creativity. The devil will try to oppose that belief and want to highlight your weaknesses and flaws; he even will have you compare yourself with others, both physically and mentally, to push the agenda that you are not what the Creator says you are. The most important thing to do is to challenge the enemy's conclusion with what the Creator says you are. In other words, if the Creator says that you are blessed with talents and potential, you should reevaluate yourself by seeing what you are good at and what you are passionate about; then, develop that ability instead of allowing it to go to waste. In doing so, you will be in total contrast to the enemy's prediction and belief about you.

Here, you are looking for evidence to the contrary. Also, if you are energized by the enemy to believe that nobody likes you, you are a liability and will never accomplish anything. You can become contrary to this label by being generous to people, even those who despise you. Render assistance when it is needed. Extend love, even to those who do not love you, first to those around you and then to others. Also, express gratitude when necessary. If you are not accustomed to doing these things, it might be a bit difficult at first, but with prayer and constant practice and believing that you can do it, it will be accomplished. Doing these things follows the principles of God, and God is bound to his Word and principles. When we follow those principles, the Creator has no other choice but to return to us what we have sown. This is simply because his reputation and his integrity are at stake. The Creator is bound to keep his word, for his name's sake.

We earn our integrity by keeping our word, and from this comes trust, and our names will be known as having integrity. David says in Psalm 23:3, "He restoreth my soul: he leadeth me in the paths of righteousness for his name's sake." This means the Creator had no choice but to attend to David's needs because he has a name to uphold, as long as we walk in his will. Doing his will is sowing good seed, for us and our generation, and also defeating the enemy's label for us. Remember that if the enemy say you can't, start doing that same thing, and you will reap your reward from what you would have sown. It is always important to remember that the word of God spoken over your life always override the enemy's label about you as long as you believe.

You can be what the enemy says you cannot be. When you help people in any way possible, whether in a small or big way, you eventually become an asset to them and also sow good seed for your return. Continuously doing good deeds will eventually change your perception of yourself and also invalidate the enemy's perception of you. Here, you are also challenging your negative belief system.

We are born with potential and must not limit ourselves because of someone else's perception of us, mainly, the enemy's. His perception of us is always false. We should always provoke what is on the inside of us to do good work. Provocation will lead to development and materialization and will eventually erupt into our reality. Our potential and abilities are unique; the Creator knows our potential and abilities because he created us with them. He expects us to believe in what he has deposited in us and to seek his guidance so that it will benefit us and his creation—and he will get the glory.

> Before I formed thee in the belly I knew thee, and before thou camest forth out of the womb I sanctified thee, and I ordained thee a prophet unto the nations. (Jeremiah 1:5)

The Creator was telling Jeremiah that before he was born, he had already blessed him with the potential to become a prophet. Whether you are called to be a prophet, a teacher, or a pastor, it won't just happen; you have to participate in the process to make it a reality. This will entail receiving instructions from the Creator through the Holy Spirit or a spirit-led mentor, studying the Word of God, and being prayerful. It is not only about receiving instructions but also following the instructions, which is an act of obedience. Because our participation is vital for our success, the enemy usually tries to interrupt our participation by discouraging us through challenges and by having us question our ability—are we really capable of becoming what the Creator says we will become? We need to guard our minds from the lies of the enemy because his lies can cause us to choose a different path, a path that contradicts the Creator's intentions for our lives.

If we look at Jeremiah's story, we will understand that Jeremiah was no different from us. He came from a mother and a father, just like us. He had his fears, just like us, but he was still chosen by the Creator. In the same way, the Creator choose us from the womb and marked us for an intended purpose.

I was at a community high school and was preparing to teach the reproductive system, when the Lord gave me the following revelation as I reflected on Jeremiah 1:5. "Before I formed thee in the belly I knew thee, and before thou camest fort out of the womb I sanctified thee, and I ordained thee a prophet unto the nation." As I reflected on the scripture, with the reproductive system in front of me, the thought came to me that even before my parents had planned for me, the Creator knew that I would be born on a particular day. With me on his mind and in his thought, he mapped out a plan for my life.

> For I know the thoughts that I think towards you, saith the Lord, thoughts of peace and not of evil, to give you an expected end. (Jeremiah 29:11)

This shows that despite the circumstances under which you were born, the Creator still has a plan and good intention for you. If we look into the mind of the Creator, we will recognize that when individuals see conception as a mistake sometimes, the Creator does not—he knew a long time ago that you and I were coming into the world on a particular date. He already made preparations and plans for our lives, with good intentions. During that time, he already knew our potential, our purpose, and our assignment, and he was just waiting on our arrival to fulfill them, with his guidance.

THE CHOSEN PROCESS

To be chosen means to be selected from a greater number. For selection to take place, there must be more than one thing or person. Let's examine this process by bringing Jeremiah 1:5 into reality. According to Eric Olson article published 24th January, 2013 states that every time a man ejaculates, approximately 250 million or more sperm are released. In a typical ejaculation, about 250 million sperm or more are released into the woman, and only one is needed to fertilize the egg.

Let's look into the mind of the Creator, who told Jeremiah, "Before I formed thee in the belly, I knew thee and before I formed thee in the belly, I knew thee." The Creator knew exactly what he was talking about. The Creator was implying that he selected you from a total of 250 million sperm or more. Being chosen from the womb has nothing to do with our parents. This shows man's limitation. We should be grateful for life because we were chosen from millions; you and I were chosen above the others, and the fact that we were chosen by the King of all kings means that we born into royalty. That is why the enemy is after God's creation—he knows that we are chosen by God, who not only chose us but also has a plan for our lives. In that plan lies the potential to be a threat to the enemy's kingdom of darkness. The Creator is the creator of life, while the enemy seeks to destroy and steal our lives.

CHOSEN FROM THE WOMB

What becomes of the millions of sperm? They were left to die because the Creator did not have a plan for their lives. The creator does not bring you into the world without a plan. As long as you are alive, there is a plan and purpose for your life, and purposes are meant to be fulfilled. There will be challenges as you seek to fulfill your purpose, but the fact that the Creator has already planned your life, way before conception, means he already made provision for the challenges that we are expected to face. When things happen to us along the way, while we are surprised, but he is not because he foreknew that.

In Jeremiah 1:6-8, Jeremiah was afraid to speak to the people. The Creator told him not to be afraid because he would command him as to what to speak, and he would deliver him. He specifically told Jeremiah not to be afraid. Again, the Creator knew that Jeremiah would be afraid, and he laid out a plan for Jeremiah to execute the task. It is important that we walk and step out by faith, knowing that the Creator is with us.

There is absolutely no reason to doubt that the Creator has a plan for our lives. If he did not have a plan and a purpose for our lives, we would have died with the other sperm. Do not make the enemy feel that you don't have a purpose. His plan is to defeat your purpose by undermining your potential, which makes you feel that you can't do anything right, which is a feeling of worthlessness.

Let's look at the natural selection to bring out the spiritual message of being chosen. The beauty about the conception process is that as soon as the sperm, which is you, reaches the eggs, a covering comes over the egg, thus preventing the other sperm from invading. The main purpose of this covering is to protect the egg, which is you. At this point, you are sealed off by him for him. Here, you are separated from the other sperm. How blessed are you? During this process, the other sperm were rushing to get into that beautiful place of protection where you were, but they could not because they were shut out by the covering, by the miraculous power of God. There is something special about you!

All of this is the working of the Creator. The other sperms died, but you were the lone survivor. The others were your brothers and sisters because they came from your father. If another sperm would have penetrated the egg, it would have not been you because every sperm has its own characteristics, qualities, and features. This means you were born to be victorious because your first victory began in the womb. The Creator started you off as a victor and a winner, and that is why he equipped you with potential and ability to continue that winning trend. You were born as a victor and not a victim—the victim mentality was not born in you. Success is your birthright. If the Creator wanted you to be a victim, he would have allowed you to die, like your brothers and sisters. He allowed you to live, so he wants you to continue to be a winner in him.

> **YOUR FIRST VICTORY BEGAN IN THE WOMB**

> **YOU WERE BORN AS A VICTOR AND NOT A VICTIM**

Let's stretch our imaginations to think of how there were millions of sperm swimming with us to meet that egg, but we swam away and left them behind. It is amazing how we swam with direction. Who was guiding us? It was definitely the Creator. He had his eyes set on us. The other sperm were swimming, but we were way much swifter than they were because purpose was attached to our lives, and we had a race to win. Remember—we have the ability to be victors because it was born in us.

You may be surrounded by negative loved ones, or perhaps you were nurtured in a chaotic environment, and you feel like a loser. Remember that a winning spirit and a winning mentality was born in you. The enemy often uses environment, people, and things, such as the media or drugs, to speak defeat into our lives. He knows we are born with the ability for greatness and success. His main intention is to reduce us from victors to victims. He does not want us to pursue victory because he knows when we pursue victory, we become confident and positive, with a high self-esteem. He seeks to silence those strengths with self-pity, fear, and guilt.

Looking into the mind of the Creator, we can conclude that he is a protector, even before birth; he protects our lives and inheritance. He is a Creator, the giver of life. He is a provider who makes provision for what we are expected to face. He is a keeper; he keeps us from conception until we finish our journey on earth. He is a refuge and hiding place, a place where we can run and hide, and he will block off anything that wants to invade our space.

Remember that the Creator started your course of life well. Trust him to guide that same life he started. He gave you life; he knows why he chose you and entrusted life to you. The founder knows why he started his foundation; the manufacture knows why he manufactured that product. Hence, the Creator knows the reason for your creation. A victor you have started, and a victor you will be unto eternity.

CPSIA information can be obtained
at www.ICGtesting.com
Printed in the USA
LVHW110500250322
714344LV00001B/88